SELLING IS SERVING

SELLING IS SERVING

Master The Art Of Selling ETHICALLY
With CONFIDENCE And CONVICTION

NICK STAAB

Publisher: Addea Media

ISBN: 978-1-7399431-0-3

The strategies in this book are presented primarily for enjoyment and educational purposes. The information and resources provided in this book are based upon the author's personal experience. Any outcome is based on the author's experience and there is no guarantee that your experience will be the same or that you will have similar results.

Although the author and publisher have made every effort to ensure that the information in this book was correct at press time, the author and publisher do not assume and hereby disclaim any liability to any party for any personal or professional loss, damage or disruption caused by errors or omissions, whether such errors or omissions result from negligence, accident, or any other cause.

Advance Praise

I genuinely cannot believe Nick's making this readily available to the public. I'll put this simply; if you take action on the information provided in this book, your life will transcend to levels you never thought possible!

There aren't many people I'm truly inspired by in the sales world, but when Nick asked me to do a little 'shout out' for his book, I jumped at the opportunity. I'll keep it short and sweet. I LOVE selling, but I've always focused on conversions. I hit a block and wanted to take it to the next level. Nick offered me one hour. It changed my complete outlook on sales, taking away the focus of SELLING and replaced it with a focus on SERVING. He broke down, what felt to me, the true secrets – what I'd been searching for. I took action IMMEDIATELY! The result? £330k in 90 minutes, with more coming in - the largest close by far!

- **Jamie York,** Aspire Property Group

Nick is a real diamond, his attitude to sales is so refreshing and he believes in truly helping people by being completely transparent. By implementing his 7 step life-changing system I grew my sales by 54%. His genuine love and passion for helping and serving others truly are infectious.

- **Ree Hurakan,** ReeAnimate

As someone who struggled with selling for years, there were times I didn't want to pick up the phone and call a prospect at all. Nick showed me a way to sell authentically that aligns with my laid back personality. Applying the strategies he has taught has allowed me to sell more confidently over the phone and to enrol more clients into my agency. My best sales call using Nick's training resulted in £2,400 monthly revenue from one client!

I highly recommend working with Nick if you are tired of struggling with the selling process and want to close more sales, without being pushy.

- **Seb Brantigan,** The Britpreneur

I first met Nick back in July 2018. I saw a raw talent combined with an amazing work ethic when he started working for us as a sales specialist at Assets for Life. I saw a fire in his belly and year by year that fire has continued to grow. Nick is now by far our best performer at selling our life changing training products and has become a partner in our business. He demonstrates that selling is simply caring about your customers, and making it about them not you. If you serve them well, the money will come as a by-product.

If you want to learn how he has been able to transform his life, take action and get your hands on his life-changing book!

- **Jay Munoz,** Co-founder of Assets for Life

I would like to dedicate this book to my family:
My mum and dad, Kathy and Paul;
My two brothers, Mark and Darren;
My four nephews, Daniel, Tom, Josh and Charlie.
Loving sales, loving serving, loving life!

Contents

PART TWO: PROCESS 97

Foreword

Nick and I started working together in July 2018. He had climbed to the top of many sales industries, and at that point, he felt compelled to explore the world of consulting for the UK's biggest trainers and speakers. Nick knew he had a gift and knowledge that he could pass on to help change thousands of lives.

By 2018 I was already making 7 figures a year in revenue and my business was on its way to becoming one of the biggest property investment and education companies in the UK.

Knowing of my industry experience, Nick connected with me and came down to my offices to meet me. At that moment, I knew that Nick was the person to give my business the injection it needed to take it to the next level.

After a good chat getting to know each other, we began to discuss possible ways for us to work together and collaborate. Within minutes I could sense that Nick had a rare talent - one that my training and event business desperately needed. I quickly contracted him to consult for my company.

Within days, Nick's teachings and ethics had made a significant impact on me and my sales team. We doubled our sales conversions in person and over the phone within a month and revenue increased by 150% and raised from £100k to over £210k. We had a 38% increase in cash collected on the day vs customers being set up on payment plans. Our lead generation was up by 44% mainly because of Nick's unique ability to create ravings fans. We got multiple referrals from each client and this strategy didn't cost us a penny and it increased total turnover by £62,000.

As time passed the impact of Nick's infectious attitude and burning desire to help others continued to spread through my company like wildfire. My team, clients, event delegates, mentors, investors and business partners were begging to be personally mentored by Nick.

Fast forward two years since I started working with Nick and my company is closing just shy of 7 figures on a monthly basis as a direct result of the work that Nick has done within my business. The true increase in sales and money being raised by my clients is almost impossible to measure but I would conservatively estimate it to be above 8 figures.

I consider myself very fortunate to have been trained and mentored by some truly exceptional people but when it comes to selling and serving I have never met anyone who can match the level of Nick's passion and integrity.

Despite the vast amount of knowledge I have accumulated over the last twenty-two years, I can honestly say that Nick Staab's training is world-class and has been one of the very best I have ever experienced.

Nick and I co-founded the Elite Sales Academy back in 2018. With my expertise in starting and growing 7 figure businesses and Nick's passion to teach others how to sell ethically, we did that with one clear vision in mind: teaching people how to sell and close ethically and do so confidently so their business and personal lives could flourish. The exact systems and teachings that our clients have invested thousands of pounds to learn are documented and shared with you here in this book.

These teachings will change your business, your income and your life forever. All you need to do is absorb it and implement it!

To your success,

Liam Ryan
Property Investor and Co-founder of Assets For Life and the Elite Sales Academy

Acknowledgements

I am eternally grateful to Dea Fileva, who helped me write and edit this book. To my loving parents Paul and Kathy who made me the man I am today. To my older brothers Mark and Darren who have always had my back. To my loving Uncles, Aunties, Cousins, Sister in Laws and my late Grandparents.

To my best friends Luke Barker, Mark Sullivan, Tony Sullivan and all my friends who supported me along the way.

To Austin Behan, Seb Brantigan, Ibrahim Braimah, Kav Coatman, David Morgan, Mathew Bigg, Kirsty Russell, Frances Moss, Tyler Simms, Katie Parker, Jon Bingham, Hadjer Beyaz, Ross Mallalieu, Rebeca Petran, Jamie York, Adam Stott, Phil Elder, Dillon Dhanecha and all of my amazing team at Assets For Life.

To my mentors Jay Munoz, Jessen James, Ree Hurakan & Matt Elwell for teaching me how to be amazing and being a huge influence to make me want to help and inspire others.

To all of my clients and the amazing action takers in the Assets For Life, ESSA, Elite Sales, Elite Closing & CAS Academies.

To my amazing business partner Liam Ryan.

To my number one fan Suz Hawkins - TT, O4L

And to all of my readers, for their interest, precious time and comments.

Thank you.

Before We Dive In

Nothing sells better than serving.

Working with hundreds of entrepreneurs, business owners, consultants and employees I see no greater power than that of being elite at sales to inspire, inform and transform lives and business. My mission is to encourage and enable you to do this easily and well.

I have watched small businesses flourish and grow and become smarter, more agile, increasingly profitable and successful. I have seen their owners gain confidence and grow their businesses, expand their income and have forged stronger teams in the business. I have also seen sales consultants become elite at selling by closing more deals, getting more work opportunities and huge commission cheques. I have also seen employees from all trades who are stuck in the rat race earning a flat income and no matter how hard they work, go on to create new careers in sales and take full control of their earning potential and live the lives of their dreams.

I am the co-founder of the Elite Sales Academy along with my business partner Liam Ryan and we are the premier Elite Sales training and education company in the UK with a growing international presence. Just to be clear, when we talk about 'Elite Sales training' we mean training individuals who master the art of sales and negotiation and only sell to clients when it is the best next logical step for them based on their problems, wants and needs.

I grew to become one of the UK's top Sales Consultants by selling for and training the sales teams of some of the biggest professionals in the UK such as Sir Richard Branson, Liam Ryan, Jay Munoz, Jessen James, Ross Mallalieu, Jamie York and many more.

In just one day of selling for a speaker on average, I would personally close high ticket deals totalling multiple six-figure amounts and take around 10 per cent commission off of the money collected. I have coached and trained sales teams around the world. I have the expertise when it comes to training new and existing Sales professionals to be elite at selling.

After years of consulting with Liam, we joined forces and founded the Elite Sales Academy on a hybrid business model. Entrepreneurs, business owners and new or existing sales professionals would pay for the mentoring and hand-holding to learn our unique system to become elite at selling. We have worked with thousands of people who have gone on to grow their businesses, achieve financial freedom and create legacies that they and their loved ones can be proud of and enjoy.

The adage that *'selling is bad'* is nonsense. The true essence of sales is *finding out what someone needs and providing it.* If you're a business owner, chances are you have a product or service. However, even the brightest products or services are useless if you can't do one thing: sell them.

There is one main reason you feel that selling is bad and that is that you have had a negative sales experience or someone has told you that salespeople are bad.

We have two innate fears which are universal and are common to all humans regardless of the society or culture into which they were born and raised. They are the fear of loud noises and the fear of falling. Any other fears we have, we learn ourselves. The great thing about learning any other fear is that we have the ability to unlearn them also.

What happens when you hear the word *'sales'*?

Most professionals I speak with have negative reactions. Their stomachs turn, their jaws tighten, they feel fear, anger or even disgust.

You may have heard the saying that "**Cash is King**", this is the slang term to say that money is the most valuable investment tool.

I say "**Sales is Queen**" because to become a King you need a Queen. You need to be able to sell to make cash. Every King needs a strong Queen by his side, right? Look at a game of chess. Your Queen chess piece is one of the most powerful and when you lose your Queen it's really hard to survive.

It's game over when you lose your King (*i.e. no cash flow, you become bankrupt*) but without your Queen (*Sales*) it's almost impossible to keep your King and survive. You could possibly survive and get by but ultimately you need to be able to sell to be able to grow.

If you are coachable, willing to learn and ready to move into a new phase of visibility and achievement then you have no excuse for not learning how to become elite at selling. You are doing your customer a dis-service if you let them walk away without having bought from you. Why is that? If a customer comes to you with a problem and you have the perfect solution and you let them walk away without purchasing it then nobody wins.

Maybe they wanted to think about it, speak to their partner, wanted to compare it with competitors, whatever the reason you have theoretically let them leave you with an open wound and either one of two things will happen. The first is that they will find someone else and exchange money for them to fix their wound who won't do as good a job as you would have. The second is that they will walk the earth longer, maybe even for the rest of their life with this open wound never getting fixed.

The main reason people can't sell and help people take the next logical step is that they are not in the position to be able to close a sale. They do not have the know-how. They do not have the knowledge, systems and procedures in place to close deals.

If you're a business owner or in sales right now you might have or sell a great product or service but you don't feel excited or comfortable when you have to ask for the money or when you get an objection. Maybe you aren't closing as many deals as you would like. Perhaps you find customers telling you that your product or service is great but now might not be the right time or maybe they want to go away and think about it. When they go away to think about it they promise you they will call you back straight and you take the word for it but you never get that phone call or hear that email notification ping. Maybe you have had times where you have gone to call a customer and you say to yourself internally "I hope this person doesn't pick up". You may even ditch the call and send them an email or a text message instead (You've just decreased your chance of closing by **90%**)

My system is proven to work in many different industries and areas including:

- Sales
- Property negotiation
- Retail sales
- Commercial

- The car industry
- Corporate
- Wellbeing
- Services
- Call centres
- Live events
- Consultations
- Webinars
- Follow-ups over the phone
- Group meetings
- Making money through selling
- Becoming better negotiators
- And many more

Having mentored hundreds of people to become elite at sales I have created a unique and streamlined process that will guarantee your success in sales which is very simple for anybody to follow. I have created hybrid ethics to train people to become elite at closing with no smoke and mirrors sales BS. Skills that not only can you implement into your business or career but also your life to have a better mindset, better relationships and a better quality of life. Being elite at selling will benefit you anywhere in the world, sales is universal and it will always be the number one skill everyone should master to help improve all areas of their life.

In this book, I will teach you how to become comfortable at selling, how to monetise and make serious amounts of cash as a business owner, sales consultant or even an employee, how the human brain operates when it comes to selling, how to manage your state, how to handle objections with ease, how to retain and upsell clients and more.

I have created a simple 3 step system for you to learn and follow. I call it the 3 P's.

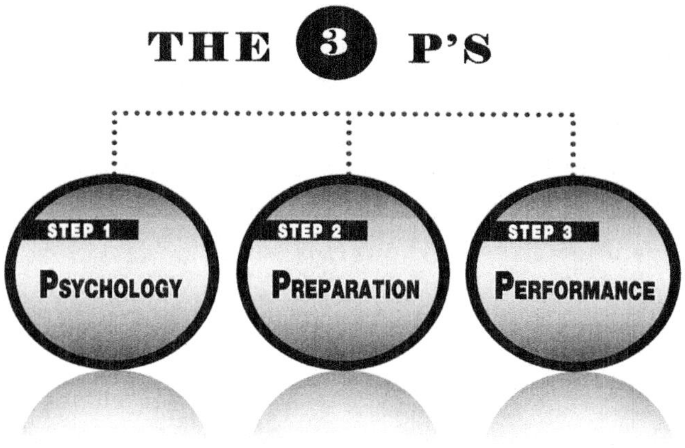

Our tried and tested processes and systems from the 3 P's allows anyone to learn and master the art of selling and become elite at it, no matter if you're already a confident closer or you feel that you have little to no experience with selling.

By the end of this book, you will have learnt the exact system that I have created and used to close over ten million pounds worth of deals and that my personal clients have used to close over 100 million pounds worth of deals.

You will even be taken through **The 7 Step Serving System** which is the complete system I use and adapt in any selling situation to sell literally anything, as long as it is the correct next logical step for your customer.

I want to forewarn you here that I am a down to earth, no bullshit, genuine person. Unlike most traditional salespeople I am not personally motivated by money. I have undertaken many personality profiling tests throughout my life and I always come out as an emotional connector (You can ask my ex-girlfriends and they can confirm I am a very emotional person). I am more motivated by helping others and it gives me a much higher sense of fulfilment than earning huge amounts of commission.

This has given me the edge to become one of the **top 1%** in my field and create a system focused on helping others and prioritising selling through emotion over logic.

The vast majority of my clients who had invested in sales training in the past found that it did not match their personality type, they found the selling to be too pushy, too hard sell, the systems that were too complicated and difficult to implement.

My ethos is to sell by serving your customers, to find them the best solution and if they are not the right fit for your product or service to help them. I am a rare breed in the sales training industry and that is what sets me apart and leaves my clients feeling confident and proud to sell in an ethical way.

Anyone can learn these techniques, it doesn't matter what type of person you are, what background, what culture. You only need two things to be able to start your journey to become an elite closer and they are:

- Your mouth
- A mobile phone

What I love about what you're going to learn is that you can implement this and sell for yourself or sell for others from anywhere in the world.

This book is like a recipe for baking the perfect cake. I will be able to give you the recipe and baking instructions that I have tried and tested to get great results. If you take it home and change the ingredients or bake it for too long then you are not going to have the same cake as me and my successful clients.

Nothing sells better than serving, but you have to be elite at it. I'm going to show you how to become elite at selling, the right way.

PART ONE

Psychology

For the first part of this book we are going to look at two types of psychology that you need to master to become elite at selling:

- Your psychology
- Your buyers' psychology

Your psychology and relationship with selling is the biggest thing you are probably currently missing right now. Even if you have the perfect system in place you will not be able to get the results if you are in the wrong mindset.

Research has shown when it comes to selling it is broken down into the following:

- **80%** Mindset
- **20%** Strategy

> *"If you think you can or you think you can't, you're right."*
>
> *- Henry Ford*

In this first part of the book, I am going to address some of the biggest mindset actions that will have the biggest impact on you closing or not closing a deal.

You are going to learn:

- How to feel comfortable when selling
- Why do we fear sales
- Why do we need to be elite at selling
- That having the right money mindset is key
- The different types of buyers
- How being certain makes a huge difference
- How we still have an primal brain
- How to manage your state
- Why do people buy from people that they like
- The different buyer personality types
- How first impressions count
- The power of a great handshake
- How a smile makes all the difference (even on a phone call)
- And more

1

Being Comfortable with 'Selling'

We typically associate the word 'sale' with something bad. When we hear the word we picture the sleazy, pushy salesperson who is looking to take our hard-earned money so they can line their own pockets.

> **According to the Oxford Dictionary, a sale is:**
> *The transfer of ownership of and title to property from one person to another for a price.*

Now here is where most people get stuck in their mindset. Let's say, I go to a shop to buy a new TV. I find a TV I like and then I exchange my money for the TV. The shop just made a sale. Right?

But what about intellectual property, patents or ideas?

They are bought and sold all the time and we never think of them being a sale. Everything we do in life is a sale and we have been learning this practice since childbirth. Since the first day on this earth, you have been selling to others.

Take a second to think about it. Why do babies cry? Every single time a baby cries it is crying to tell you something, to influence you to do something.

The baby will sell you the idea that they are in pain, that they are hungry or that they just need some love and affection. The baby is not doing anything wrong. It's just using a simple mechanism that helps them get the results they want. It is simply there because it is effective.

As we grow older, so do our brains. We eventually learn to talk and structure conversations and our arguments become more and more sophisticated.

At some point, we sold to our parents or guardians that we would be 'good kids' in exchange for some ice cream or to watch our favourite movie. We wanted to sell this 'want' or 'need' to our parents and hey if that failed we could always fall back on our first sales skill of turning on the waterworks until we got what we wanted.

Sound familiar?

As we grow older we sell our ideas and wants all the time.

I lost count of the number of times I made promises to my parents in order to get something I wanted in return.

"Dad, let me wash your car for £10"

"Mum I'll go over to the shops and get the bits you need if you let me get some sweets with the money left over."

Everything is about a sale and the older we get the more aggressive, pushy and persuasive we can get. We tend to emotionally argue more and manipulation is one of the strongest human techniques in existence.

"Get me that job and I will do ANYTHING you want"

"If you leave me I'm afraid I might do something stupid"

Some extreme, but very practical examples.

This is all active selling. You can spot this kind of selling with some experience of being on the giving or receiving end. But there is another form of selling that is almost impossible to spot and it affects each and every one of us in different ways.

Indirect Selling

Have you ever wondered why the typical man really cares about the watch they wear or the car they drive? Or why can a typical woman spend countless amounts of her hard-earned cash on beauty products?

When these people buy a new watch, car, dress or makeup they make an indirect sale.

In a nutshell, we basically do this because we want to sell ourselves. Like I said earlier, wanting to sell something isn't necessarily bad, It's what we are wired to do. We are all different and we all have our own level of moral compass. For some of us, there can be no sale immoral enough to perform. Look at a drug dealer for example. Now I believe selling drugs is very immoral but besides that, it is extremely net-negative. It's risky, dangerous and there are by far easier long term ways to make money.

Why We Need To Be Elite At Selling

Selling is so fundamental to our existence. Take a second and try to think of a single case of someone doing something without having a sale in his or her mind. You can't, can you?

Being good at sales is critical in every life sector. If you can sell your ideas to others you can persuade them to do almost anything you want. If you know that your product, service can help your buyer fix their problems and reach their goals then you can do this with 100% confidence. You should always try to provide your customer with as much value as possible for what you sell. In the long run, you will get higher sales conversions, have fewer cancellations, repeat customers and build credibility in your industry that will drive clients in your direction.

Most of the business professionals I worked with would look to hire someone to do the 'sales' for them but the problem was, they would need money to be able to do that. So they faced the choice of doing jobs they didn't really like or to try and get good at sales.

Here is the truth, When you decide to work for yourself and be your own boss and do something that you are passionate about you must learn to get good at sales. Not just good at it, you need to love it and make it the main core of your focus because everything you do in your life is a sale.

- When you convince a customer to buy your product by informing them how it will fix their problems and help them achieve their goals in X time - **SALE**
- Convince your partner to go to the new Oriental restaurant that opened in town by reminding her how much she loved the 'Hong Kong Sweet & Sour Prawns' and had told you it was one of the best things that they had ever tasted when they last had a Chinese - **SALE**
- When your child is refusing to eat their carrots and you convince them how it will help them to be able to see in the dark - **SALE**

Pretty much everything we do to influence people to get them to do what we want is a sale.

Why Do We FEAR Sales?

FEAR = **F**alse **E**vidence **A**ppearing **R**eal

Perhaps when you have gone to sell your product or your service you get nervous, You label yourself as someone who "can not sell".

I can guarantee at some point in your life you have had a negative sales experience. Someone has been too pushy, made you feel bad or tried forcing something down your throat and this has left a sour taste in your mouth.

Think back to a time when you bought something or were being pushed to buy something. Maybe you went ahead and bought just to get the salesperson to stop but you immediately got cold feet and cancelled after the transaction and got a refund. How did that make you feel?

Not great I imagine and we tend to let these experiences frame our view of *'sales'* or *'selling'* to be negative.

Remember that we are not born with a fear of selling. We were taught it by our loved ones, teachers and we probably experienced a time where someone who wasn't skilled in selling left us feeling bad.

A client and now a good friend of mine Seb Brantigan used to FEAR selling for his online marketing business. He had an amazing product but like most business owners he doubted his abilities and he was scared of coming across as pushy, he struggled to ask his clients for the money. After investing in himself and becoming an Elite Sales Specialist he now makes more working two months part-time than he used to in one year.

Using Affirmations To Become Elite At Selling

Affirmations are usually seen as positive but actually, you can have negative affirmations that will eventually turn into negative beliefs. Any thought that is repeated enough will eventually become your belief.

Have you ever heard of the statement:

"Breakfast is the most important meal of the day?"

You have probably heard this term in your life but did you know where it came from? Perhaps you have probably been told this by one of your teachers or maybe you have had it passed on by your parents.

Interestingly, before this notion came about, breakfast wasn't a particularly important meal. People didn't have specific "breakfast" foods and ate whatever was lying around or leftovers from dinner the night before. Our ancestors ate a small meal and ate the larger meal when it was more convenient during their farm work. The line "Breakfast is the most important meal of the day" was invented in the 19th century by Seventh Day Adventists James Caleb Jackson and John Harvey Kellogg to sell their newly invented breakfast cereal.

A lot of research has been done to prove that breakfast is not the most important meal of the day, yet the belief that we hold all over the world is that breakfast is the most important meal of the day. This belief spread around the world from a marketing campaign.

If we keep repeating negative affirmations to ourselves when it comes to selling then we will eventually believe them and we will lose out on opportunities to help more clients take the best next logical step.

Right now you may be saying the following to yourself:

- I'm no good at selling.
- I hate selling.
- I don't have enough value to help other people.
- I cannot charge more money as my competitors are charging less.

These statements are what we call affirmations. We use affirmations all day long and they are typically negative. Most professionals consciously or unconsciously use these affirmations whenever they are in a selling situation. There are simple ways to change your beliefs and what you tell yourself, you need to focus on using one simple technique to bring positive affirmations into your life.

Affirmations become habits. If you say something over and over, it's likely to stick. Think about when you repeat a behaviour several times. You get better at it, right? The same thing goes for affirmations, whether they are positive or negative.

Let's say you aren't confident at selling and you wish to improve this. Your belief is probably that you're not good at sales. Instead of continuing to focus on your weakness, flip the statement around and say, *"I'm improving my sales skills every day."* This allows you to take a negative statement and turn it into a positive affirmation.

Watch as your beliefs begin to change. Remember, incorporating more positive affirmations into your life doesn't have to be hard. To make your affirmations or statements more positive, try setting reminders of your affirmations on your phone. These can be positive statements about you and areas you wish to improve in.

Some examples of the affirmations I practise daily to keep me positive and motivated:

- I am adventurous. I overcome fears by following my dreams.
- I feed my spirit. I train my body. I focus my mind. It's my time.
- I am in charge of how I feel and today I am choosing happiness.
- I let go of all that no longer serves me.

Some examples of the affirmations I practise daily to make me elite and serving and selling:

- I bring all my energy when serving my clients so I can solve people's problems by offering them the best solutions.
- I love waking up every morning as an Elite Sales Specialist as I get to work with my favourite customers and I know this will change their lives for the best.
- It doesn't bother me that I can charge more than my competition because I know that I provide 10x more value than them to my customers.

Every time my reminder pops up on my phone, and I see a positive affirmation pop up, I smile. It truly changes the way my day goes, and my overall outlook on life. Try creating positive affirmations now and setting them to come up as reminders throughout the day.

> A ***goal*** will get you somewhere.
> An ***affirmation*** will make you someone.

Summary

So now you know that being able to be elite at selling is an amazing gift. I want to remind you that to help you move forward I no longer want you to think of it as selling, I want you to think of it as influencing. By benefiting others, you will benefit yourself.

Action points to take away from this chapter:

- Learn to become comfortable with selling
- Be aware of indirect selling
- Know the importance of being able to sell
- Be conscious of why we typically fear sales
- Practise positive affirmations

EXERCISE

Before moving onto the next chapter, take some time to make a list of all the times you have influenced someone to take action and the amazing things that came from it for them and yourself.

2

Money Mindset

A money mindset is an overriding attitude that you have about your finances. It drives how you make key financial decisions every day. And it can have a big impact on your ability to achieve your goals. If you change your mindset about money, you tend to make better choices about how to overcome challenges.

The power of positive thinking really does matter when it comes to being successful and elite at selling.

Network = Net Worth

> *"You are the average of the five people you spend the most time with."*
>
> *- Jim Rohn*

When it comes to money in particular, this is the killer.

Some of us are spending time with people who are earning nowhere near what we want to earn. Now the sad reality is that some of those people are people that we love.

We are the average of the five people you spend the most time with:

If you hang around five broke people, you're going to be number six.

If you hang around five negative people, then my friend, you're going to be number six.

If you want to be making seven figures, start hanging around people who are making seven figures. If you want to be closing more deals, start hanging around people who are closing more deals. If you want to attract better people in your life, start hanging around the kind of people you want to attract.

In school, they teach you: 'do not copy others.'

In the business world, this is the worst advice ever.

Get around successful people now, follow successful people on social media.

Please understand there are drains in your life and there are radiators. Drains will suck the life out of you because they're projecting their own crap onto you. Radiators will lift you up and warm you up. In a nutshell, they'll bring out the best in you.

On your journey to becoming an Elite Sales Specialist hanging around the right people is a simple implementation that will change your life forever. Now, it's very important that this includes your clients as well.

Do not hang around people who drain you plain and simple, it's very very important that you understand that.

I'm not telling you to divorce your partner or cut off your family, just be mindful of who you are surrounding yourself with and who you allow yourself to give your energy to.

So, how else can you control your environment and who's around you?

Social Media is a powerful tool and in this current tech age, it's important that we don't get stuck being a consumer online and that we become producers.

Here is an exercise you can implement right now to start surrounding yourself with successful people right now.

Go to Facebook and join networking and support groups relevant to your interests or areas of business you are in or that you would like to get into.

If you are not in the *Assets For Life Elite Sales Community Facebook* group, I suggest you join it now. We have created a free support page to help people grow into Elite Salespeople: www.facebook/groups/elitesalescommunity

You can surround yourself with like-minded motivated people, ask questions, learn new things and hear success stories from clients getting real results by implementing the simple changes from our system.

You sell how you buy

I remember my first part-time job while going through college working in the Mens' department of my local TK Maxx clothing store. It always baffled me when I was working on the fitting rooms and a customer would try on a shirt, tell me it was great but then give it back to me because he wanted to shop around in case he found something else. Then I would see him again days later purchasing the exact same shirt.

I would think "If you like it and you have the money, why wouldn't you just buy it?"

I really couldn't get my head around these types of people but I learnt over time it's because I naturally make buying decisions very quickly.

The types of people I couldn't understand are typically the buyers who spend hours researching, comparing and negotiating prices and have what is called a non-supportive buy cycle, which is one of the biggest and most common weaknesses a business owner can have. How you buy is how you accept other people will buy and therefore how you sell. If someone has to do lots of research, haggle on price or whop around to find the 'perfect' thing then they are more likely to accept it when their prospects want to do the same thing.

People who make quicker buying decisions are better able to help their prospects make faster buying decisions. However, if we meet the 'I want to think about it' type prospects in a buying situation and we don't push back when they want to compare more proposals or features it will impact our chance to close and it will lengthen your sales cycle.

> *95% of our purchase decisions take place unconsciously.*
>
> *- Harvard Professor, Gerald Zaltman*

What was the most expensive thing you ever bought and how did you go about it?

Did you spend hours comparing, haggling the price, or delay the decision so you could look up more information? Or did you do enough research to make an informed decision, find something in your price range that fixed the problem and just buy it?

A non-supportive buy cycle makes us more empathetic towards procrastinators, price shoppers, comparison shoppers, researchers and price objectors who are hot and cold, in and out, stall, put off, make excuses, outright lie and tell sad stories. Whatever the reason, if you aren't someone who makes quicker buying decisions you will naturally agree with them and waste a lot of time and energy following up on a lost deal. Even when your gut was telling you the business was lost and they were not going to buy from you.

Are delay tactics the only symptom of a non-supportive buy cycle? No.

Let's say you are the type of person who likes to research prior to making a major purchase. These days with the power of the internet it is so easy for us to search for options, features and pricing so easily at our fingertips.

If you're currently in sales have you ever presented all the information to a prospect of what you do, how you do it, how it will fix their problems and then how much it will cost them to have them say 'Wow! That sounds amazing! Let me just think about that and get back to you.' They go away and never reply to your calls, emails and pleas.

If you fall victim to prospects that are conducting research it can cause you to prematurely present information before you ask your prospects enough questions to know if they are a qualified, good fit and that your product will be their solution.

If you don't qualify your prospect and get them to visualize the solution your product will give them then why would that prospect ever speak to you again?

What real value did you bring?

How was what you told them different from any of your competitors out there?

There are many types of non-supportive buying cycles. To see if you typically support a non-supportive buying cycle ask yourself the following questions:

In your life would have you invested in your own professional development, or waited for your employer to pay for it?

How is that impacting how you sell?

Do your prospects push back on your price, looking for a less expensive alternative, no matter what the "value" you have preached to them is?

Do they need to do their "due diligence" before they can buy from you?

When your buying process aligns with and supports the desired sales cycle, then the obstacles that used to stall you and stop the process become small delays that can be handled and worked through. As well as knowing how your prospects buy, you need to know how you buy yourself. If you support a non-supportive buying cycle all is not lost. It's important for us to be aware of the different types of buyers we will come across. I have created **The PASS Buyer Blueprints** which list the main four.

The PASS Buyer Blueprints

There are typically four different types of buyers' blueprints and learning the PASS model will give you clarity on your relationship with spending and it will give you a massive advantage to adapt to other people's buyer types when closing in sales situations.

Penny Pinchers

Penny pinchers are typically people who are not willing to spend their money and they only really ever buy things when they are on sale. They can be known to be hoarders who don't like to throw anything out unless they might 'need it one day'. They will typically feel like there's not enough out there for them. They don't like to talk about money and when they do it's typically to complain about how expensive something is.

Penny pinchers can be a challenge to sell to as they have a very dominant mindset where they want a discount or something for free.

Avoiders

Avoiders are people who avoid looking at their bank accounts and financial statements. I see this with a lot of business owners I have worked with. The way they keep the pulse on their business is by logging into their business bank accounts, crossing their fingers, saying a few prayers and hoping when it loads up there's some money in it.

Avoiders typically believe they don't deserve to make money, they self sabotage their financial lives. The thing is the more they avoid looking the more their anxiety goes up and they will typically complain and worry about money a lot.

Spenders

Spenders are people who like to spend. They are primarily focused on buying material things and to feed this need they use the money they have in the bank and if they don't they will go and find it somehow. Spenders will typically consume more than they produce and spend more than they can afford and are often in debt.

Growing up, I knew a lot of people who had flash things but they were always in debt. For a spender, their self-worth is attracted to their net worth and the funny thing about that is that they try to spend a lot to replenish their self worth and they get stuck in a counterproductive cycle.

Savers

Lastly, we have savers. Savers are money conscious people who typically live a balance of having a life today and making a living in the future. They have a high value of security and tend not to invest much, if they do it's typically in a low performing ICER or a low performing savings account. 'Better safe than sorry', 'slow and steady wins the race' are their typical mottos. Savers typically think that leveraging money through credit is a bad thing. They don't typically own credit cards but if they do they feel like they should be paying off as much as they can as fast as they can so they don't incur any interest.

I look at it like this, If I were to spend £1,000 on my credit card to buy some stock or to pay for some mentorship that would make me £2,000 then what do I care about the interest I pay? It would not be over 100%, I will make loads more money than the interest so it's worthwhile using debt to leverage.

A saver would not look at it in the same way, they would think the more that they save the more that they will have which is technically true in their minds however if your money is saved and not working for you then it's actually depreciating over the years. One pound now will not be worth the same in 10 years compared to what it is now.

I say you should look to save at least 6 months of living costs in your personal account and 6 months of business running costs in your business account but anything over that you should look to invest and get it working for you.

So of the 4 types of buyer blueprints which one are you most like?

- Are you a penny pincher?
- An avoider?
- A saver?
- A spender?

I think that most of you are a blend of them all with some traits higher than others. It's important to know how you buy and also how your customers buy so that you can adapt to their needs and beliefs to ensure you have a higher chance of selling to them if they are the right fit.

I have created a fifth buyer blueprint that hits the sweet spot of where you need to gravitate your buying mentality towards. I've found that the perfect buyer blueprint is the Investor and they sit between a Saver and a Spender. I have created the following graph to break this down further.

Investors

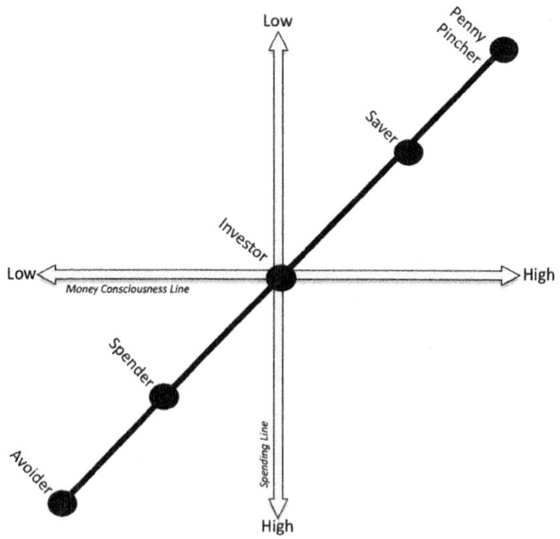

An Investor is somebody who spends when it is the best logical step for them and who will save until they find the best solution. An investor is not a gambler. Investors are people who are looking to get a return on their investment. They want customers to spend with them, but they really want them to understand exactly what they are getting so they can confidently implement our solution to help them fix their problem without feeling any remorse down the line.

I believe having the mindset of a penny pincher or an avoider won't really help you, that's why they are the furthest away either end of the quadrant. If you're in the mindset of an investor and you identify that a customer is a penny pincher then you could meet them at their level and highlight the long term savings of your product or service. An Investor is a chameleon who can move either end of the quadrant and influence their customers to make the best logical decision.

Summary

Hanging around the right people and having the right mindset around money can be a simple mindset shift you can implement from today so see massive changes in your business and personal life.

- Be aware that your network = your net worth
- Be aware of how you buy will determine how you sell
- Learn the 4 PASS buyer Blueprints
- Work on distributing the focus of your money mindset to the areas that serve you best between **P**enny Pinching, **A**voider, **S**pender, **S**aver
- Adopt the Investor buyers blueprint

EXERCISE

Before moving onto the next chapter, take some time to learn what buyer blueprint you naturally adopt and start to practise on learning which ones your clients may adopt. You can practise this with your team, colleagues or family and friends.

3

The Human Brain

The biggest problem I find right now is so many sales trainers and so-called professionals who are out there giving people the wrong impression around selling.

They portray magic hacks, manipulation, getting clients to buy your product they never wanted.

Most people think to be good at sales you need to become a typical sleazy salesman. They think that the process needs to be funky and portray smoke and mirrors but in reality, this really isn't the case.

What you do need to do is SERVE your client. Serving is selling. All you are doing is working out if the client is a good fit for your service or product.

Being CERTAIN

When you are selling from a place of certainty within you and you are totally certain that as long as your client wants and needs your service or product enough and you are certain that your service or product will be the solution to their problems then you will be selling with confidence.

Remember these two words, as long as you are in service you are selling.

> *"There is no greater gift than a service to others."*
>
> *Nick Nolte - Author/Actor*

The easiest trick to learn to become better at selling is to end the mindset that says you are trying to sell to someone. This is what you have to stop thinking if you want to come across as genuine and feel confident in your approach.

Your first job is always to serve your client or prospect. If you are in service that person will connect with you in that place and there is no trying, fancy tricks or smoke and mirror surprises. You are being a coach and asking the right questions to uncover the pain and working out a solution to fix the problems. You will allow your clients to come to their own realizations, they might have a light bulb moment about issues they had never consciously thought about before. You will never tell a client how bad their life may be or how bad their problems sound, you will simply ask the right open questions and be a good listener to uncover the problems. This information will later be used to help the client have a 'call to action' which I will cover later in this book in greater detail.

In one of the original Star Wars movies, 'The Empire Strikes Back' there is a powerful scene where Luke crashes his spaceship in a swamp and his mentor Yoda is coaching him on how to use the force and move objects with his mind. He previously taught him how to move stones with his mind but now is tasked by moving the huge spaceship out of the swamp using his mind. Luke states that moving stones is one thing, but moving a spaceship is a completely different thing! Yoda goes on to tell Luke "Only in your mind is it different" Luke then says "ok.. I will give it a try" to which Yoda responds "NO! Try not, Do, or do not. There is no try"

There is no trying, you have to be yourself and help your client move from where they are currently stuck. They are coming to you because they have a problem and if you have the solution and you or your service is the right fit for the client then they will want to have whatever it is you are offering. So you do not need to try, you need them to realize that you are the ideal person to help them if your product or service is the right fit.

I cannot stress this enough. Being confident in your product or service and showing this in your tonality when in a selling situation will position you as a trustworthy expert. Always be honest and transparent from the get-go and your customers will respect you so much more for it.

The Primal BRAIN

Before we go into a selling situation we need to use our **BRAIN** and be aware that our clients will subconsciously be using theirs too.

Benefits - What are the benefits?

Risks - What risks may be involved?

Alternatives - What other alternatives may be available?

Intuition - What is my intuition telling me?

Nothing - What if I do nothing now and choose to revisit this later?

Most people trying to sell suffer from hindering thoughts, they have internal conflicts and suffer with procrastination. You can be in one of two states, certainty or uncertainty.

There are roughly over 8 billion people on this planet right now. One-third of people across the world are currently sleeping right now, how many of the people awake do you think are worrying right now?

When you are in a selling situation that can be a real worry for you. So you need to ask yourself, what is worry and anxiety?

One of the easiest ways to understand this is that your brain is made up of two parts. There are two of you in your mind. One of them is your ego-mind which is your earthly representative of you and operates from a place of fear. The other is the real you, which is you being free of ego.

There have been surveys done that show how many people live in their real mind and how many live in their egoic minds. A whopping 96% of people live through their egoic mind and just 4% of people live free of their ego. To be in the small 4% you have to be born that way (which is extremely rare) or you have to undertake a shift in your mindset.

Your egoic brain is located at the back of your head and this is your primal brain. You have probably heard of Fight/Flight/Freeze which is the three states our brains would operate in to survive the harsh climates and threats for thousands of years. The fight-flight-freeze response is your body's natural reaction to danger. It's a type of stress response that helps you react to perceived threats, like an oncoming car or growling dog.

For the people living in this egoic mind which is 96% of the population, our mind is typically full of worry, anxiety, anger, depression etc. Your egoic self is operating externally.

In a sales situation, the mind is looking outside of itself to try and identify threats. It is trying to look into the future and predict what is going to happen in the future and it is worried about what might happen next. When you are in a sales situation most people in this egoic state are thinking about what might go wrong and when this happens your body releases a high dose of adrenaline and cortisol into its system.

Have you ever experienced something like a car accident? Or a situation where something goes wrong. This kicks off in our primal brain the Fight/Flight/Freeze response and can leave us shaking.

If we are operating from our primal brain when we go to make a sales call then we are nervous and expecting the worst. Objections from the client purchasing our product, thinking they may be dissatisfied or ask us questions that put us on the spot.

These thoughts stop a lot of sales people from even making calls, they worry so much about being in this state so they think it's best to send the client an email or text message instead of making the call. Choosing to speak to a prospect over email or message opposed to picking up the phone to have a conversation is like pouring water into a sieve. You are never going to have a quality flowing conversation, use your tonality and sell in the moment over an email. An email exchange could go back and forth over the course of hours or even days, that is if the email is even opened in the first place.

FUN FACT

Only 24% of sales emails are opened.

Takeaway - Pick up the phone and start dialling. Your chances of closing a deal over the phone or in person are over 14x higher.

The Power Of State

You need to be able to control your state, this is the first thing you need to do to be elite at selling. You are frightened and uncertain and you are trying to look for certainty. So even if you have an amazing strategy and a great script, if you are in your primal mind you will make the call badly because you have negative emotions attached to the call, you may not even make it all. If you attach negative emotions to a call that doesn't go to plan you can tell yourself *'doing that call was worse than I thought, so I won't do anymore today'.*

The trick is to learn how to change your state. You could rapidly multiply your chances of success if you take away the fear and replace it with certainty.

The State Scoring System

I have created the Elite Scoring System for my clients for them to implement before going into a selling situation whether it be a phone call, meeting or speaking on stage that has been able to boost their sales conversion rate by 46%.

My private client Jamie York who has a property training and coaching business implemented the system I am about to show you to manage his state before a sales presentation to a group of individuals. He closed £330,000 in 90 minutes and increased his sales conversions by 387% compared to the prior 90-minute sale he had done before.

Have you ever gone to make a phone call to someone and as the phone rings had that internal hindering voice saying "I hope they don't answer.' You go on to sigh with relief when you hear the voicemail message and you drop them a text or email instead.

As mentioned earlier we have a much greater chance to serve people by speaking to them rather than relying on messaging so it's key that we check in with ourselves before we enter a sales situation.

Five minutes before you enter a selling situation you need to check in with your state and score yourself between 0 - 10 with how you feel about making the call or going into the meeting. 10 is "I am pumped and so excited! I can't wait to get in there and serve this client" and 0 is "Oh my goodness I am so scared! I want the ground to swallow me up".

If you are anything below an 8 - 10 then do not make the call or go into the meeting, you need to work on your internal certainty before entering this selling situation so that's why I created **The 4 I's Cycle** to implement to bring yourself to anything an eight and above.

The 4 I's Cycle

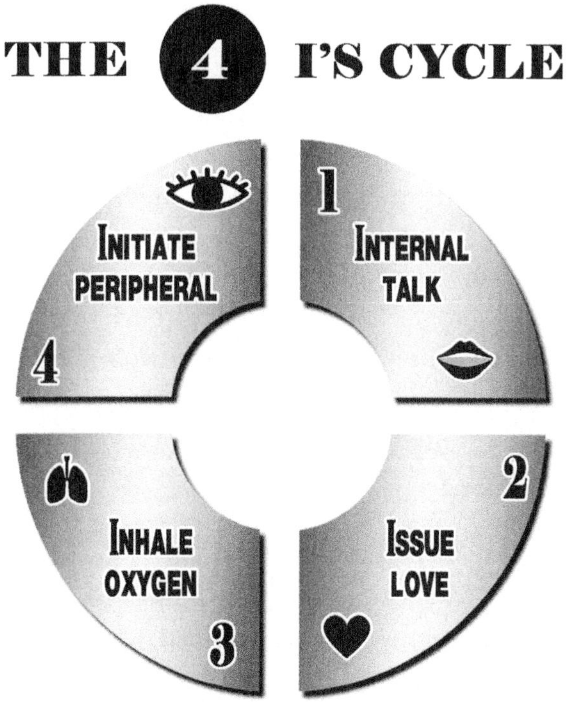

Internal Talk

The first step of **The 4 I's Cycle** is to boost yourself up you need to have an **I**nternal talk with yourself and tell yourself "I know whatever happens here that I can deal with this situation, I have a great product (or service) and if it will help solve my client's problem then it is my mission to serve this client". That is going to give you internal certainty.

Take a moment to practise this now and feel the power.

Issue Love

The second step of **The 4 I's Cycle** is to send your client some love. In this current age, it is really simple to find your client online even if you have never met them before. You can search for them on LinkedIn or Facebook. Look at a picture of them and send them some love and tell them that you are going to serve them today. Now I'm not saying to start stalking them and looking through their holiday photos from a couple of years ago but when you know what your client looks like you will feel 37% more confident.

Inhale Oxygen

The third step of **The 4 I's Cycle** is to oxygenate to improve your state by regulating your breathing using a simple technique. We breathe unconsciously all the time but when we consciously breathe and our focus goes into our breath and when you do that you can't be thinking about what might go wrong so you have shifted your mindset. Repeat the following cycle 3x to notice a difference. Get into position by sitting upright on a chair and then breathe out.

1. Take a deep breath in and suck your stomach in, you should feel your chest filling and sticking out
2. Count to 5 seconds
3. Blow the air out and push your stomach out
4. Repeat

This oxygenates your brain and pumps adrenaline through your whole body.

Take a moment to practise this now.

<u>Initiate Peripheral Vision</u>

The last step of **The 4 I's Cycle** is to initiate peripheral vision. This is a very simple technique that can help you get into, as NLP experts call it, the ideal state.

The Technique:

1. Pick a spot above your eyeline in front of you. Keep focusing on that spot, taking in all the colours, textures, light/shadow and really focussing in. Keep going for about 20 seconds.
2. Now allow your vision to extend slightly, so that you are looking at the spot and about 30cm on either side, slowly take your vision out a little more

and more until you can't focus on the spot, but you can see your hands if you stretch your arms out levelled with your shoulders.

3. Now stretch your vision even wider. Stretch your awareness in your imagination to as far around you as you can. Now you're in peripheral vision.

Take a moment to practise this now and feel the huge power of being in peripheral vision.

Now you have completed **The 4 I's Cycle** check in with your state and if you are above an 8 then pick up the phone and dial, if not then repeat the cycle from the beginning.

Summary

The human brain is a powerful one and only when you truly understand the power of being certain and understanding how we are all naturally hard-wired by our primal brains, can we start to become a master of our own and others when selling.

Managing our state before entering a selling situation can be pivotal and on average increase our chances of success by 46%. By following the state scoring system and checking in with ourselves before we enter a selling situation and getting ourselves above an eight out of ten is a game-changer.

The 4 I's Cycle is something you can easily adapt before entering a selling situation. In fact, you can use the 4 I's in so many other areas in your life outside of selling to be in control of your state and increase your chances of getting better results in anything you do.

EXERCISE

Before moving onto the next chapter, take some time to practise the 4 I's Cycle. You can practise with a team member or a friend or family member or you can think about a sales call you have made in the past.

4

People Buy From People They Like

It's a popular saying in business circles, but it holds true: People do business with people they know, like, and trust (especially in sales).

No one wants to hand their money to some faceless corporation or sign a contract with someone they just met.

Whether we realize it or not, we want to buy from people we can trust. People who do what they say, fulfil their promises, and fix things when they go wrong.

This is as true of people as it is of a company. In their journey, prospective buyers want to know they can trust the company as much as they can trust the individuals they're dealing with.

That means the trust-building starts from the outset, when they first encounter you at a conference, visit your website, or read one of your emails.

The Sales Framework Timeline

There has been an evolution in the sales framework that salespeople have followed through the recent years. Consumers have adapted to being sold to and being left with negative sales experiences so most companies have adapted to this, but our Elite Sales Specialists are at the top of their games and way ahead of the majority of sales professionals. There is a timeline I have created to outline the evolution of the salesperson.

THE SALES FRAMEWORK TIMELINE

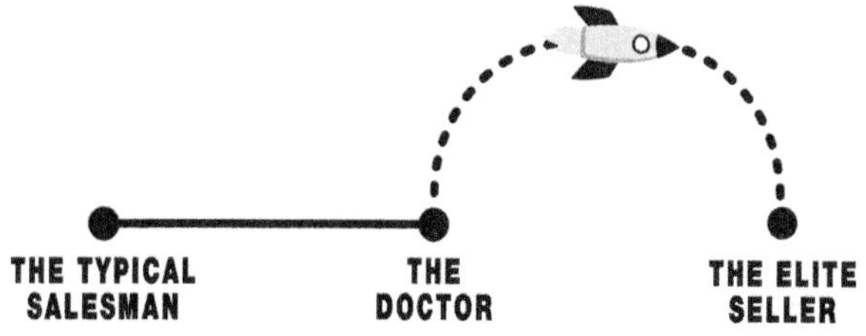

The Typical Salesman

At the start of the timeline, we have the typical salesman framework which is what has given salespeople a bad name in the current day. This style of selling is loud and enthusiastic and can be very pushy and forceful by using tactics and tricks to get a customer to buy a product or service that they probably didn't need or that won't solve their problem. This didn't bother the salesman as they only cared about making money and it leaves buyers with a phenomenon called 'buyer's remorse.'

Perhaps you have been talked into buying something that sounded great but when you used it you realised it didn't solve the problem you had or lived up to the promise that it had made. Maybe you were mis-sold and when you woke up the next day you felt angry and upset that you made this purchase.

The Doctor

Most salespeople in the current day follow the Doctor's frame as people start building up resistance to being sold to by the typical salesman. Salespeople who follow the Doctor's frame try to be less intense than the typical salesperson as they don't want to come across as obnoxious. They focus on the symptoms and the problem with this is that they don't tend to get to the root of the customers' problems. Focusing on the symptoms may provide a short term fix but it most likely won't be a long term solution.

The Elite Seller

The last framework that I would suggest you adopt is to have the framework of an elite seller. Very few salespeople know how to do this properly and they make up a small percentage of the market and close and serve way more people than their counterparts. An elite seller will not try to provide solutions until they uncover all of the problems and qualify that their solution is the best next logical step for the customer to solve the root of their problems. If our solution is not the right fit we look for alternatives and provide the best next steps for the customer, even if that means working with another competitor if it will help solve their problem.

The Elite Seller is more like the doctor than a typical salesman but they are much better listeners and are able to dig deeper and let our customers have realisations or lightbulb moments that they may have not previously comprehended. When we solve problems they have a long lasting effect and we help our customers get from where they are now to where they would like to be a lot faster, safer and have it be as stress-free as possible.

We dont tell our customers the solution, we help lead them to come up with the solution themselves so they can truly understand what we offer and the life changing benefits they will receive when they take action and implement our product or service.

The opposite of remorse is satisfaction and we ensure our buyers are left with buyers satisfaction over buyers remorse. This will result in little to zero refunds, customers who will give you amazing reviews and endorse you to others and will be more likely to buy from you again.

HEAD Personality Profiler

Now you have the framework of an elite seller. It's so important to know your personality type and that of your potential customers if we wish to sell at an elite level and be able to serve all different types of people.

I have undertaken and invested into lots of different types of personality testing such as DISC profiling, Myers Briggs testing, Insight, GEM Mastery™ and many more to help me master the different types of personalities. Some experts will say there are twelve different types, some say eight and some four. I have created the HEAD Personality Profiler for my clients which focuses on personalities and it is focused heavily towards buyers patterns. The HEAD Personality profiler consists of 4 types of personalities which makes this easier to remember and implement.

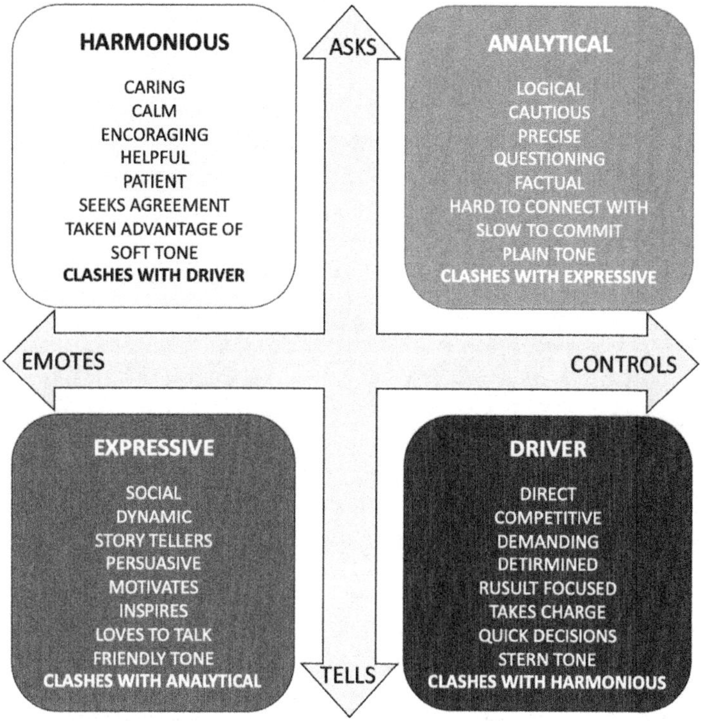

Harmonious

The first personality profile is **Harmonious**, people who fall into the harmonious personality are more likely to be calm and caring individuals. They are always going out of their way to help and encourage others and they are patient. They seek approval from other people and have to be very careful that their kindness is not taken advantage of. They are known to speak softly and they can clash with people who have a Driver personality.

Expressive

The second personality profile is **Expressive**, people who fall into the expressive personality are more likely to be social and dynamic individuals. They like to be seen and heard and make great storytellers. They are great at motivating and inspiring others and can be very persuasive when trying to influence someone. They have a friendly tone and they can clash with people who have a Analytical personality.

Analytical

The third personality profile is **Analytical**, people who fall into the analytical personality are more likely to be very logical minded and can be cautious. They are very precise and like to know all the facts and they will question everything before making a decision. They can be hard to connect with and very slow to commit to something new. They can talk in a plain, boring monotone and they can clash with the expressive personality type.

Driver

The fourth and final personality profile is the **Driver**, people who fall into the driver's personality are more likely to be more direct when speaking to others and they are very competitive, they love being the number one in everything they do. They are very determined and results focused and like to take charge when working with others. They are quick to make decisions, can speak in a very stern tone and they can clash with the harmonious personality type.

We are typically made up of all four of the HEAD personality types, two of the four personality types are significantly higher than the other lower types, and of the two that are higher we have one that is predominantly higher. Ask yourself what personality types you fall into the most.

Become A Chameleon

It's important to know which personality type we fall into and to understand why we are emotionally wired like we are. People buy from people that they like or look like and when you have the ability to know what personality types other people hold and adapt yours to mimic theirs then you can have much deeper connections.

When you know the personality types of your customers and you start to use the same language and tone as them, then they will feel that you think like them. If you speak like them, you think like them.

For example if you're speaking with someone who has an analytical personality and you go in with the expressive personality type overtalking and trying to inspire them they are probably going to tell you that they want to go away and do their own research and think about it. If however you're speaking to someone analytical and you hit them with some facts and data they will feel more comfortable that they are speaking to someone who knows their stuff and they will be more likely to see you as an expert and listen to what you're offering without the need to go away and 'think about it' themselves.

Another example is if you imagine speaking to a Driver in the Harmonious personality type. If they are soft spoken and trying to seek agreement from a driver they will not get very far. If you adapted to be more of a leader and were direct to the driver they would be more likely to respect you as the expert and buy from you.

If you want to increase the chances of a customer buying for you then you are going to have to become more of a chameleon. You don't want to be listing every benefit of your product or service to a customer but if you focus on the benefits that match a customer's HEAD personality you will build a stronger connection. For example, give harmonious people encouragement that they can benefit from your product easily, an expressive person a client success story, an analytical person with accurate data and a driver with the results they will get from using your product or service.

I have been able to highlight some key points to think about when dealing with people in the four different personality types.

How to sell to a Harmonious:

- Listen to them
- Be very friendly
- Create a relaxed atmosphere
- Demonstrate how you or your offering have helped other people
- Be calm and trustworthy
- Be constructive
- Give them a two choice close and explain what you think is the best option

What irritates a Harmonious:

- Overconfidence
- Hard sell
- Pressure
- Confrontation

How to sell to an Expressive:

- Friendly attitude
- Appealing to their good nature
- Involve them
- Get them talking
- Give them choice
- Hit them where they are enthusiastic

What irritates an Expressive:

- Providing too much detail (they get bored easily)
- Pestering them
- Being too direct
- Talking at them

How to sell to an Analytical:

- Demonstrate your knowledge levels
- Show you are credible
- Beck up everything with evidence
- Use facts and figures
- Give them time to commit

What irritates an Analytical:

- Hard selling
- Over promising and under delivering
- Asking for too much personal information
- Too much talking

How to sell to a Driver:

- Be direct with them
- Make punchy statements
- Talk to them about results
- Discuss objectives
- Show results/proof

- Demonstrate your knowledge
- Stroke their ego

What irritates a Driver:

- Waffle
- Too much talking
- Over friendly people
- Not getting to the point

It really is worth thinking about your clients and working out which are their dominant behaviours. If you can put your driver hat on when speaking to a driver you will strike a much better rapport and increase your chances of them buying from you.

As you are now aware that people like people who are like them, another ace up your sleeve is to dress like them. A harmonious person tends not to wear flash clothes, an expressive person tends to like bright colours and bold hairstyles, an analytical person tends to dress very plain and drivers love to dress sharp in colours like red or black.

Summary

It is important to understand that people naturally buy from people that they like. There is a **Sales Framework Timeline** that identifies how Elite Sales Specialists are way ahead of typical sales people these days.

To become elite at selling you must understand the personality types of yourself and your prospects. The HEAD personality profiler is a great way of learning and mastering this. To truly influence others you must identify their personality type in buying situations and become a chameleon yourself and adapt to it.

EXERCISE

Before moving onto the next chapter, take some time to learn what personality type you adopt. Practise with a family or friend who may have a different personality type to you and test using the 4 different personality types with them and look out for how they will positively and negatively respond to each one depending on the personality type.

5

First Impressions Really Do Count

First impressions are key in sales whether it be in person or over the phone. While it may not seem fair to place such an outsized impact on someone's first few words or one's appearance in a first interaction, our brains are simply hardwired for efficiency, and first impressions are crucial.

You need to be on your A-game right from the moment that they see or hear you because this is when your customers make subconscious decisions about you.

At a dinner recently a good friend of mine Katie told us a story about an experience she had recently whilst she was shopping for a new mattress. Now, this wasn't just any mattress; this was a high-end mattress that she wanted, which retailed around £1,500. Prior to making the purchase she had done extensive research online and had narrowed her focus to a few brands and styles. She found exactly what she was looking for at the first furniture store she visited and the price was right.

But she didn't make the purchase.

Instead, she drove all the way across town to visit another furniture store where she met sales representative Gwen. There, she purchased the same mattress she had seen at the other store. When I pressed her she admitted (while trying not to look at her husband) that she paid more at the second store than the first.

"*Why would you do that?*" I asked.

She responded: "*The guy at the first store, I think his name was Ray, just didn't impress me. I mean, from the first moment there was just something about him I didn't like. So even though he had the mattress I wanted I decided to shop around some more. Gwen, the rep at the other store, was different. Even though we had just met I could tell she cared about me. She made me feel important.*"

We all make instant judgments when we first meet people. Those judgments, which are both imperfect and emotional, have a lasting impact on how we view and interact with others.

Trust me, your prospects make these same imperfect judgments about you every day. First impressions are about likability and likability is the gateway to building emotional connections with your prospect. Emotions drive sales. If your prospect likes you they will be open to answering your questions, engaging in a conversation about their needs and situation, and ultimately buying from you.

Unlike trust, being perceived as likeable or unlikeable occurs in mere moments and begins in your prospect's subconscious long before they are aware of how they feel about you at a conscious level.

FUN FACT

40% of sales go to the vendor that responds first
Takeaway - Responsiveness is a key skill in sales. However, keep in mind that speed alone is not good enough. You have to be quick while providing a QUALITY response (i.e. answer all your prospects' questions).

How To Be Likeable

According to the Oxford Dictionary to be 'likeable' is:
Having qualities that bring about favourable regard.

We all, to some extent, have qualities and characteristics that make us naturally likeable to certain types of people and personalities; though at the same time we possess qualities that make us naturally unlikeable to others.

The problem we face in sales is we don't always get to choose the people we interact with. Many of the people we encounter will not be naturally attracted to us. Complicating things more are the preconceived notions that all people bring into relationships. These perceptions, which include but are not limited to cultural, racial, and socioeconomic biases, are also beyond our control.

There was just "something" about Ray that Katie didn't like. That "something" could be that he reminded her of a bully back in school, a bad date in college, or a sales rep that broke a promise in the past. Perhaps she didn't like his facial expressions, his accent, tie, eye contact, posture, or the tattoo on his wrist.

The point is, there are a myriad of reasons a prospect may not like you and many of the reasons (rational or irrational) are completely outside of your control. This is why, when you meet new prospects, it is absolutely critical that you control those things that are within your power to control.

Take Control of Perceptions

There are, however, important and critical actions you can take that will positively impact first impressions and likeability. These actions are completely within your control and, when executed properly, help you both neutralize biases outside of your control and attract people who might not otherwise find you naturally likeable.

Smile: A pleasant, sincere smile is the best way to make a great first impression. The smile is the universal human language and people are naturally attracted to people who are smiling. So be aware of your facial expression and put a smile on your face.

Be Polite: I saw a bumper sticker once that said, "Mean People Suck." People who are rude, impolite, and discourteous are unlikeable. Unless you were raised in a barn by animals, someone taught you basic manners. Put those manners to work in all interactions with prospects and customers. People will notice.

Dress: Despite the admonition "Don't judge a book by its cover," people do and will judge you based on what you wear, drive, and your grooming and appearance. If you engage in face to face sales conversations, dress well. Wear the best and most professional garments you can afford. Ensure that they are cleaned, pressed, and put you in the very best light.

Grooming: Look your best. Ensure that you smell good (breath – BO) and that your cologne or perfume is not overpowering. Ensure that your hair, facial hair, and nails are clean, cut, clipped, and manicured. If you have tattoos, cover them up. Yes, tats are more acceptable in today's society than ever before however, they can potentially turn off buyers who don't consider them appropriate. "I chose not to buy from that sales rep because he didn't have a tattoo," said no one ever.

Stay Focused: In today's demanding work environment it is easy to become distracted. Jim Rohn once said, "*Wherever you are, be there.*" This is essential advice when it comes to first impressions. You must develop the self-discipline to shut everything else out and remain completely focused on your prospect.

Be enthusiastic: Enthusiasm for your product, service, and company is what sells. Enthusiasm is transferable and infectious. Your enthusiasm is driven by your attitude and beliefs, so it is critical to work consistently to build and retain a winning attitude. One note, though: there are few things more off-putting than insincere enthusiasm; so be careful not to get carried away.

Be confident: Weak people repel. Arrogant people are turn-offs. Confident people attract. Confidence is driven by your self-image, product knowledge, attitude, style of dress, health, and even your spirituality. This is why, even if you are an inside sales rep, it pays to dress for success. When you look good you feel good. Your level of confidence is a direct reflection of your willingness and self-discipline to invest in yourself.

Why First Impressions Are So Vital

Although you never get a second chance to make a first impression, you only have to make a good first impression once to build a profitable relationship with your prospect.

The good news is, making a great first impression is actually very easy if you focus completely on what is within your control.

When it comes to making first impressions, research shows us that when we meet someone in person for the first time we make impressions in just a quarter of a second and when we speak for the first time over the phone it takes just 4 seconds.

In that time your customers will subconsciously decide:

- If they can trust you
- What kind of person you are
- If you sound convincing
- If you are an authority
- If they want to do business with you

This is why it is so key to manage your state before a meeting or phone call as it could be the difference between a deal or no deal.

The Power Of A Great Handshake

When meeting people face to face a powerful tool you have at your disposal is that of a handshake. The history of the handshake dates back to the 5th century B.C. in Greece. It was a symbol of peace, showing that neither person was carrying a weapon. Since then it has been a gesture that is implemented to build trust and connection between two parties. It can be an amazing rapport builder if done correctly however, if not done well it could have the opposite effect and make someone lose trust in you.

There are 3 handshakes you need to look out for:

1. **The Wet Fish** - a limp wristed handshake with little to no grip and no eye contact
2. **The Crusher** - an uncomfortably over the top squeeze with too much eye contact
3. **The Elite** - using a firm pressure with good eye contact and a natural friendly smile

Think about the last time someone shook your hand like a wet fish, they had a weak grip and they looked off to the side avoiding eye contact with you.

- Did you like them?
- Would you buy from them?
- Could you trust them with your children?

Take a moment to think of a time you received a phone call from someone softly spoken and with very low energy. Were you compelled to have a great conversation with them?

Now think of a time someone who has shaken your hand with the crusher grip. Taking the upper hand and staring you out aggressively.

- Are they aggressive?
- Do you feel natural around them?
- Would you feel comfortable being around this person?

Try to think of a time you had a call with someone being loud and aggressive. Did you feel compelled to stay on the phone or were you thinking 'how do I get this person off of the phone?'

Finally, take some time to think of someone who shakes your hand like an elite seller. They give you a firm but natural pressure with good eye contact and a warm welcoming smile.

- Do you feel comfortable?
- Are you open to engaging with them?
- Do you trust them?

Think of a time you had a phone call which was pleasant, friendly and informative where the other person really listened to you. The call made sense, had a purpose and left you feeling good. This is the phone equivalent to the elite handshake.

Put That Smile On

It's extremely important to smile when selling. You should even smile when talking to buyers on the phone because your facial expression changes your tone of voice. But smiling actually has a much deeper impact. It's not just about seeming agreeable, or showing confidence in your product, or not looking like a grump. As behavioural and psychological research demonstrates, there are good, non-obvious reasons to smile when you're in a selling situation with customers.

Smiling at a person triggers psycho-physiological effects in them that are pretty much automatic. There are two of these effects, and they act together to improve your buyer's state of mind. And when people are in a good state of mind, they're more willing to listen favourably to you.

The dual benefits of smiling

Mirroring

Studies show that human beings tend to mirror the behaviour they see in others. Thus, when you smile at buyers – even if neither of you has said anything particularly funny – they are moved to reciprocate.

Expression triggering emotion

Psychologists have found that causation between facial expressions and inner emotions runs both ways. It's not just that a pleasant feeling causes somebody to smile. It's also that when a person smiles, it tends to create a pleasant feeling in the person.

So when you smile at the buyer, two things happen, both of which are good: The buyer mirrors your smile by smiling themselves, and that smile alters the buyer's inner emotional state for the better and you want buyers to be in a good emotional state when you present to them.

Trying to sell to someone who's in a bad mood – who's nervous, upset, irritated, or afraid is really like spitting into the wind. These moods change buyers' judgments, and even their perceptions.

There's actually one other aspect to consider: the effect on your own mental state. When you smile or laugh, you feel better too. The smile triggers positive emotions, including optimism and confidence. Optimistic, confident salespeople win more and bigger sales.

Psychologists have written countless articles about the benefits of smiling. Smiling makes us feel good which also increases our attentional flexibility and our ability to think more holistically.

Smiles Over The Phone Are Unseen, But Most Definitely Heard

Question: If a smile widens on a phone call, and no one is there to see it, does it make a sound?

As it turns out, it does.

It's a fact that people can hear a smile through the telephone. When your smile can be heard, chances are you convey the right image, the one your customers expect and appreciate, the one that helps you establish a rapport.

Human beings can differentiate vocal intonation not only between a smile and a non-smile but among different types of smiles. Smiling affects how we speak, to the point that listeners can actually identify the type of smile based on sound alone.

Smile prior to picking up the phone as you want to be in "pleasant mode" before you know who is calling, rather than afterwards. Smiling after the call has commenced changes the tone of your voice. Your tone of voice is a key factor, 85% of the message when dealing with disenchanted customers/clients. Smiling adds warmth to your voice and is a critical factor to the success of a customer service representative's call.

The company Nestle places branded mirrors at each phone rep's station so the reps can see if they are smiling when they are talking on the phone.

Another method I teach my clients is to paste simple reminders on computer monitors or on the phone itself with messages like:

- Are you smiling?
- Shoulders back, smile and dial.

Personally, I find it helpful to stand up and move ar important calls — it instantly changes the energy my voice. A smile should be the foundation of all of your sales conversations and calls.

FUN FACT

92% of all customer interactions in sales happen over the phone and it takes an average of 8 cold call attempts to reach a customer.

Takeaway - Prospecting is hard and most of us hate it. But if you give up on a prospect after too few attempts, you are passing up a potential sale. Be persistent and determined.

Summary

You may be feeling overwhelmed to remember all of this, remember that practice makes permanent and it will come. Remember that becoming elite at selling is a marathon and not a sprint, if you focus on working on one technique at a time and mastering it you will subconsciously add it to your routine actions.

What I love about mastering perception is that when you start to practise using this in your personal and work life with people around you, you will notice the difference in your relationships, agreement and influence on other people. You will be a better communicator and have much better relationships.

TIP

Make a note of all the things you need to do in order to make a first impression and stick it on a wall or around your monitor. Have a pre-sale checklist listing all of them that you can get into your unconscious brain before the meeting or the call.

EXERCISE

Before moving onto the next chapter, take some time to think about the different perceptions and trial them with a friend or family member. Try giving someone the wet fish or crusher handshake and to talk without smiling and then with smiling and hear the difference.

PART TWO
Process

For the next part of this book, we are going to work on the sales **PROCESSES** before we look at performing **The 7 Step Serving System**.

To become elite at closing you need to look after yourself as an elite being. Your health, diet & mindset have a huge influence on how you perform in selling situations.

If you don't look after yourself properly, you will not function properly.

I am going to show you my 40-minute daily routine that myself and my elite closing clients practise daily to stay on top of our game.

There are 3 things that I look for in every sales conversation and they all need to happen for me to get the best result for me and my customers. I'm going to teach you these 3 simple things to master and execute with ease in any sales situation you encounter.

Research has shown when it comes to the perfect selling balance between a sales consultant and a customer it should be a mix of the following:

- **80%** of the time the customer speaks
- **20%** of the time the consultant speaks

To get our customers to speak four times more than we do, we need to ask quality questions and become great listeners. I'm going to teach you all of the different types of questioning to get the information you need as well as to build solid trust and rapport.

There is a **LOT** of money to be made from being elite at selling. In this part of the book, I am also going to teach you the many ways you can monetise the skill of being an elite seller to live the life of your dreams.

> *"Learn from yesterday, live for today, hope for tomorrow. The important thing is not to stop questioning."*
>
> *- Albert Einstein*

You are going to learn:

- The power of practising daily meditation
- The effects of gratitude
- How exercising for just 10 minutes can have powerful effects
- The effects of cold shower therapy
- The 3 Q's system - Qualification, Question, Quantify
- Types of quality questioning
- The ARQ framework which you can use to control a sales conversation
- The 3 routes of monetising in sales
- The Elite Sales formulas to calculate your income
- How monetisation is more than money
- And so much more.

6

The 4 M's Method

If you owned a Ferrari, you wouldn't fill it up with cheap fuel. So if you want to be elite at selling and closing, you need to treat your mind and body like a well-oiled machine.

Affirmations are usually seen as positive, but you can actually have negative affirmations that will eventually turn into negative beliefs. Any thought that is repeated enough will eventually become your belief.

> *"Patience, persistence and perspiration make an unbeatable combination for success."*
>
> *- Napoleon Hill*

A Healthy Body and Mindset is the biggest factor that can ensure you are operating at your highest potential and it will ensure you allow yourself to achieve maximum success in your business and life.

I have a vast amount of knowledge and experience from selling in the health and fitness industry and I have invested vast amounts of time and money into some of the top mindset coaches in the UK and US. I have also spent a lot of time in Thailand, Cambodia and Vietnam in 2019 visiting monasteries and learning the traditions of Buddhism.

My experience allowed me to create a bespoke system for myself and my clients that I call The 4 M's Method. The beauty of this system is that you can start implementing this system immediately and seeing massive results right now, with very little effort or prior experience. You can implement it into your daily routine and it will just take 40 minutes to complete.

THE 4 M'S METHOD

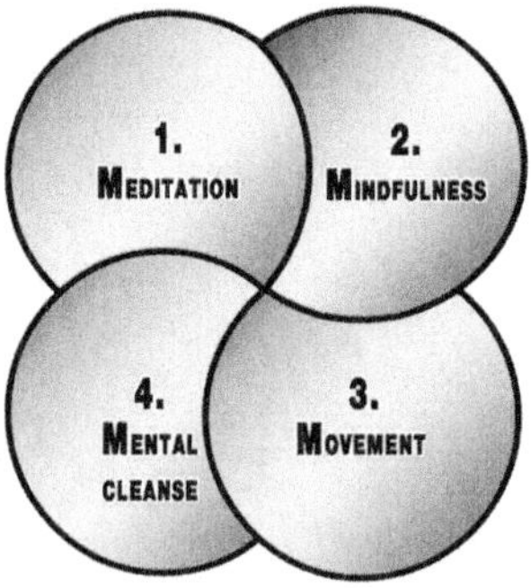

The 4 M's Method works in a 4 step order and if repeated daily it will heighten your chances of success and fulfilment for a lifetime. For the next part of this book, I am going to

break The 4 M's Method down in the timeframe to envision that you would normally sleep for 8 hours and would aim to go to bed at 23:00 and wake up at 07:00. You can adapt the times accordingly to your schedule and lifestyle.

Implement these 4 steps to your morning routine and you will have increased energy, build better relationships with your clients, close more customers and bring more success into your business and life in general.

Prelude

The first step of The 4 M's Method will be the first thing that you do when you wake up. Well, you will probably need to use the bathroom first (which is allowed) but the reason I say the first thing is because many of us have a bad habit of falling prey to checking our smartphones every morning. In fact over half of the UK population fall victim to this.

Did you know that 52% of people in the UK will check their phone after they wake up before doing anything else? If this is a habit you have, then you are not alone and preparing yourself correctly the evening prior will ensure you get the most out of this system and the benefits it has on your mind and body.

The evening prior you will need to put your phone on airplane mode at least 30 minutes before you go to sleep and then you will not activate it again until you have completed The 4 M's Method. As well as the impact not using your phone until you have completed the morning routine will have, it is really important to not be in the habit of using your phone before bed.

Here are the 3 main reasons to put the phone away before you drift off.

1. It keeps your mind psychologically engaged

   Smartphones were designed to make our lives easier. They are designed to give us information and entertain us but when it's time to turn the lights off and go to sleep the last thing our brain needs is more information or more entertainment. Even a quick check can engage your brain and prolong sleep. What makes this habit worse is feeling the need to constantly be connected and available. A lot of us feel the need to immediately answer, respond, post or scroll. The smartphone era has forced us to feel like we can never really 'log off', even when we are sleeping.

   Going to bed should be a happy, peaceful and relaxing experience and engaging with your phone too close to bedtime can negatively impact those feelings.

2. The 'blue light' suppresses melatonin

   Let's cut to the chase. The blue light that your phone emits is not only bad for your vision, but it's bad for your brain too. Research has found a correlation between suppressed levels of melatonin and exposure to blue light. Melatonin is a hormone responsible for controlling your sleep-wake cycle and when your body runs low on it, you can experience insomnia, tiredness throughout the day and irritability.

The blue light from your phone is an artificial colour that mimics the daylight. This can be great in the day as it can make us feel more alert, but this is the opposite of what we need at night when we are winding down for bed. Viewing the blue light from your phone screen disrupts your body's internal clock and rhythm and thus decreases the quality of your sleep.

3. The alerting properties delay REM sleep

You probably know what it's like to scroll through Facebook or Instagram before bed and see something on there that makes you upset or that triggers a nerve. Even if you were to see something happy right before bed this can trigger a response that prolongs falling asleep which consequently delays REM sleep. These emotions can leave you staring at the ceiling for hours feeling wide awake.

Our smartphones are supposed to make our lives easier but what it does if you use them before bed is the exact opposite. It's distracting you, keeping you awake and stimulating your brain thus delaying your REM sleep.

So now you know the negative impacts of using your phone before bed. I will ask you to make sure your phone goes on airplane mode and out of sight. The phone will then not be taken off of aeroplane mode and used until you have completed The 4 M's Method.

Let's get into **The 4 M's Method.**

Step 1: Meditation (Duration - 10 minutes)

Meditation has been a common practice for thousands of years now. Some archaeologists date meditation back to as early as 5,000 BCE. The reason it has been practised all over the world and is a staple art of many cultures and religions is because of the life-changing benefits it can create. Here are the 3 main ways incorporating daily morning meditation will massively improve your mindset.

1. **Meditation reduces stress.** When you are stressed your body releases cortisol. Cortisol promotes depression, anxiety, blood pressure, fatigue and brain fog. I'm sure we have all experienced these symptoms at some time or another when we have been overworked or stressed in our jobs or businesses. If you do not regulate cortisol you will burn out and feel anxious. Meditation is one of the best things we can implement to reduce our stress and limit our cortisol production. A recent study was done at the University of Oxford where 50 people with chronic pain implemented daily

meditation. After 8 weeks, 94% reported feeling less pain and having experienced lower levels of depression and anxiety.

2. **Meditation enhances self-awareness.** Meditation will help you become the best version of yourself. You will be able to gain more control of your thoughts and be able to steer those to more positive patterns.
3. **Meditation helps lengthen your attention span.** Before I started to meditate I would struggle with brain fog. I had a difficult time remembering people's names, famous actors in movies. Since I worked on meditation the brain fog and difficulty remembering things disappeared.
4. **Meditation helps improve sleep.** Did you know that over half of the world's population suffers from or has suffered from insomnia in the past year? Insomnia doesn't mean you just can't sleep, insomnia can be when you try to sleep you can't shut down and your brain starts having racing thoughts. Meditation can have a massive impact on lowering insomnia.

Now we know all the benefits, let's talk about how easy meditation is to add to our daily routine.

I have found that doing just 10 minutes every morning as soon as I wake up while I am relaxed and I have not been distracted by my phone is the perfect duration to get the desired results and optimise my available time. If you would like to do longer than 10 minutes then you are more than welcome to.

Find a peaceful, quiet location where you can relax and sit on a chair with your spine upright. Find a relaxing soundscape or 10-minute meditation session online. Really focus on your inhalation and your exhalation when you breathe and you will have times where thoughts come into your mind and you forget you were meditating. Just remember this is normal and the purpose of meditating isn't to block everything out, it is the ability to be able to control your thoughts and coach them along. Your brain is like a muscle so this is like working it out. The more you practise and implement meditation the easier it will become for you.

I found the Sam Harris App on iPhone and Android was groundbreaking for my meditation journey when starting. He offers a free 28-day challenge where you can follow his 10-minute guided meditation where he will teach you how to meditate. The beauty of the app is that you can download the sessions in advance and still play them without your phone needing internet data, so you can ensure you have no tempting phone distracting before starting your meditation session.

Step 2: Mindfulness (Duration - 10 minutes)

The second step of The 4 M's Method is to practise mindfulness. As human beings, we look for things to be grateful for. We have an primal part of our brain that I mentioned earlier which is designed to protect us. We naturally go out of our way to look for active threats so we can protect ourselves from harm. Since our ancestors walked this earth we were being hunted, we had to endure harsh weather conditions. We were always in danger of dying so our mind has programmed itself to look for threats to protect us from. Whether it is escaping from predators or finding shelter to protect us from storms, we got accustomed to unconsciously always scanning our environment for potential threats.

If we don't look for things to be happy and grateful for, it can be unnatural for us to feel positive and grateful.

If you drive a car, think back to when you first started driving this car. Remember the make, the model and the colour.

I bet you started to see more of your car on the road than you ever noticed before.

Do you think they were not there before?

They were always there, our brains would just not register them.

Five years ago a group of scientists conducted a long term group experiment to observe this phenomenon over time. They took a group of forty students who just graduated from Harvard University and split them into two groups.

They would study their lives and make all of the participants follow a strict guided routine with just one difference.

- *Group one had the added daily task of doing just five minutes of gratitude writing each morning.*
- *Group two would have all of the tasks of group one without the gratitude writing.*

Five years later the researchers gathered both of the groups and reviewed their brain activity and looked at how their lives had turned out and the vast majority of people in group one displayed healthier, stronger brains and were in better-paid jobs, had better financial success and personal lives compared to the vast majority of people in group two.

For step two of the Monumental Morning Method, you will just be writing three things you are grateful for and one major win from the previous day. I try to pick things that are very outside the box and all around us and find something different each day. Rather than generic ones try to be creative and think outside the box. How about being grateful to smell your favourite freshly ground coffee, the ability to give back to a charity, the power you give back to help others. You can get really creative and outside the box with these.

I follow up the three things I am grateful for with one big win from the previous day. For example:

1. *I served John and helped solve his problems and closed him on my top £25,000 mentoring package.*
2. *I had one hundred fifty people attend my webinar and 53% of the attendees have booked a follow-up consultation call.*
3. *I had a powerful meeting with my team and we made a lot of plans and actions to scale the business.*

Once we incorporate this habit as part of our daily routine we will be finding more things in our lives to feel grateful for which gives us greater levels of fulfilment and makes us perform better in our businesses and serve more people. After writing our gratitude list we move onto step 3 of the Monumental Morning Method and we are ready to get sweaty.

Step 3: Movement (Duration - 10 minutes)

Once my mind is primed and ready to take on the day it is time to get my body there too. I will do a resistance workout throughout the day most days but step three of The 4 M's Method will have you incorporating a HIIT workout.

Working out releases good hormones which keep us driven and focused to take on the day as well as giving us a wide range of health benefits too.

HIIT training stands for High Intense Interval Training and it will typically range between ten and thirty minutes. I personally found the magic sweet spot is fifteen minutes to get a great benefit and be time-effective for my lifestyle but feel free to do slightly less or more time if you require. Just fifteen minutes of HIIT can give us massive benefits to our body and mind.

HIIT involves short bursts of intense exercise alternated with low-intensity recovery periods. Interestingly, it is perhaps the most time-efficient way to exercise.

For example, a HIIT workout using a stationary exercise bike could consist of 30 seconds of cycling as fast as possible against high resistance, followed by several minutes of slow, easy cycling with low resistance.

This would be considered one "round" or "repetition" of HIIT, and you would typically complete four to six repetitions in one workout to take you up to fifteen minutes. I like to get creative and do something different each and every day using just my body weight.

Here are 5 key reasons why HIIT needs to be in your morning routine.

1. HIIT can burn a lot of calories in a short time
2. Your metabolic rate is higher for hours after the exercise
3. It helps you burn fat & strengthen muscle
4. HIIT will improve oxygen consumption
5. HIIT will lower blood pressure, blood sugar and resting heart rate

There are many ways to add high-intensity intervals to your exercise routine, so it isn't hard to get started.

To begin, you just need to choose your activity (running, biking, jumping, etc.).

Then, you can experiment with different durations of exercise and recovery, or how long you are performing intense exercise and how long you are recovering.

Here are a few simple examples of HIIT workouts:

Using a stationary bike, pedal as hard and fast as possible for thirty seconds. Then, pedal at a slow, easy pace for two to four minutes. Repeat this pattern for fifteen minutes.

After jogging to warm up, sprint as fast as you can for fifteen seconds. Then, walk or jog at a slow pace for one to two minutes. Repeat this pattern for fifteen minutes.

Perform squat jumps as quickly as possible for thirty to ninety seconds. Then, stand or walk for thirty to ninety seconds. Repeat this pattern for fifteen minutes.

For extra guidance and motivation, I recommend you sign up for an online virtual membership where you get countless videos to follow. You don't need to join a gym or splash out here. I invest a little as £15 per month into websites like Beachbody On Demand or Peolton to follow a 15-minute HIIT workout. Try and get creative, you could even follow this by doing a walk/fast pace walk or even swimming.

Once we have finished our fifteen minutes of HIIT training we should feel hot, sweaty and full of feel-good hormones. This allows us to perfectly follow up with the last phase of the Monumental Morning Method which is a treat to follow up our hard efforts by embracing something magical.

Step 4: Mental Cleanse (Duration - 10 minutes)

So it's time for the last step which is to have a 10-minute shower but why do I call this the mental cleanse you ask? I call it the mental cleanse because you will be embracing a cold shower instead of a hot one.

Now hydrotherapy has been around for thousands of years and it can have such powerful effects on your mind and body. I have been embracing cold showers for 2 years now and the benefits I have noticed have been amazing. You may have heard of Wim Hoff 'The Ice Man' who recently popularised this phenomenon but scientists have also been able to back up the benefits from switching to a cold shower will have on your mind and body such as the following.

- Increased mental toughness
- Releases endorphins
- Lowers cortisol & depression
- Improves blood circulation

- Helps build natural resistance to common illnesses
- Heightens metabolism to burn more calories

Now I don't expect you to just jump straight into a cold shower when you have only ever been used to having hot showers. The best way to adapt to a cold shower is to shower as normal but 2 minutes before the end to turn the temperature down and gradually increase the amount of time until your entire shower is a cold one. Take deep breaths to regulate yourself and trust me when you finish your shower you will feel electric, especially after following the entire Monumental Morning Method.

Another person who is a big believer in Cold Therapy is Tony Robbins. Tony has a 45-minute ice bath every morning and there is not one day he ever wants to endure it but he shares a brilliant quote when asked about the subject.

> *"I do not negotiate with my mind, I am in control and I tell it what I am going to do".*
>
> *- Tony Robbins*

I'm sure we can all agree that Tony Robbins uses discipline as a driving force and does not negotiate with his negative thoughts and because of this he has become very successful.

Now a cold shower will not be as intense as an ice bath so you will be able to work it into your daily routine and it will not kill you.

Summary

Follow The 4 M's Method and start it from tomorrow and you will feel the benefits to your mind and body that will shine onto your business and ability to be the best version of yourself.

Aim to practise The 4 M's Method daily:

1. 10 minutes of **M**editation
2. 10 minutes of **M**indfulness
3. 10 minutes of **M**ovement
4. 10 mins of the **M**ental Cleanse

EXERCISE

Before moving onto the next chapter, make a plan to implement the 4 M's method as part of your morning routine tomorrow, or if you have the time and you're in the right place, give it a go now!

7

The 3 Q's

In every sales conversation, I do three things that need to happen. I call these the 3 Qs.

tep 1: Qualify

You must be 100% certain that the conversation you are having with your client is relevant and of interest to them and it has a possible outcome that's linked to the product or service you are offering. Once they are clear that they know what you stand for and you know that you have something they might possibly need then it's time to move onto the next step.

FUN FACT

At least 50% of your prospects are not a good fit for what you sell.

Step 2: Question

The biggest mistake over 94% of salespeople do across the globe is that they talk about themselves, how amazing their product is and all the people they have helped. If you're explaining, you are losing. Start by asking questions about them like:

- What made you come toward me?
- What problems are you currently facing?
- What have you tried before?
- What happens if they don't solve this problem?
- If there was one thing we could do together that would solve your problem, what would it be?

If your client starts asking how it works early on and you start to tell them before you know their situation and what they need then you are going to start making presumptions about them to give them information that you think they will need. This leads to problems as when you assume then most of the time you are going to be wrong. Telling is hard-selling, asking is smart selling.

> *"Assumption is the mother of all mistakes"*
> - Mr. Eugene Lewis Fordsworthe

Never ASSUME, because when you assume you make an ASS out of U and ME.

Step 3: Quantify

Once I have qualified and questioned the lead I need to move onto the last Q which is to quantify the next logical step. I see so many sales professionals not locking down the next steps with their customers.

- "Let's touch base soon."
- "Call me next week sometime."
- "Here's my business card. Get in touch."

If the client was a good fit I would say:

> "I really enjoyed our chat, I want to send you some information on the basis of what we just said. When can we speak again? I've got next Tuesday or Wednesday?"

Based on their answer from the choice close I would then lock in the appointment via a Google Calendar link so your name pops up on that day in their calendar. I then follow up with the 60-second rule with a text message or voice note to say:

> "Hey, great to speak just now. I've sent you an email with further details. Save my number to your phone and give me a thumbs up when you've got it."

If the person was not the right fit for you and the logical next step for them was to find another solution to their problem because you knew that you would not be able to help them then now is the time to disqualify them. This is one of the hardest things most salespeople have to do. They like to think they can help anyone and everyone or maybe they want to try and hard sell someone into their product or service knowing that it probably isn't the best logical step for them.

This creates two big problems:

Number one is that they fill their diaries and sales slots with people they have no chance of closing. They could have prioritised speaking to more qualified leads who were more likely to buy sooner rather than waste their customers and their own time.

Number two is that they may hard sell a client into doing the deal and they will get buyers remorse straight after which will leave an unhappy customer, ruin all possible future business opportunities and could result in negative reviews and press against you or your business.

Learning to say **no** to people who aren't qualified may be challenging for most business owners and sales professionals but it is one of the most vital things you must do to be more ethical and serve more of the right people so you can close more deals and prioritise your time.

This is how we create a flowing pipeline where we have a lot of customers moving in a direction that leads towards doing business with you. Not everyone is going to flow to the end of the pipe. We may need to take some people out of the pipeline if it is not logical to move them to the next step of the buying cycle. Keeping them in or trying to push them through your pipeline is only going to create a blockage.

Summary

These are the three steps that have to happen during any sales conversation.

Firstly if we do not properly qualify our leads then we may just be wasting our own and our prospects' precious time.

Secondly, an Elite Sales Specialist speaks 20% of the sales conversation and listens for the other 80%. You must ask good quality questions to ensure that your prospect is speaking five times more than you are.

The last step is to quantify the next steps with our prospect, something that is so overlooked in the sales world.

EXERCISE

Before moving onto the next chapter, take some time to learn the 3 steps and practise a roleplay selling situation and using the 3 Q's with a team member, colleague, family member or a friend.

FUN FACT

Here are the top ways to create a positive sales experience, according to buyers:

- *Listen to their needs (69%)*
- *Don't be pushy (61%)*
- *Provide relevant information (61%)*
- *Respond in a timely manner (51%)*

8

Quality Questioning

One of the most important parts of sales is questioning. The better you are at asking the right questions, the more understanding you are of your prospects' needs and therefore giving you the best chance to offer the right products or services to them.

Open-Ended Questions

As we aim to come from a place of serving most of the questions we ask will be open-ended questions. When we are on the phone with a prospect we want to adopt the 80/20 rule.

- 20% speaking
- 80% listening

The best way to ensure we can get the prospect to open up and be comfortable to talk for 80% of the call is to ensure we ask them quality open-ended questions.

So why do we ask open-ended questions?

- To gain information
- To show an interest in your prospect
- To make them more comfortable
- To build rapport
- To be thorough
- To get your prospect to talk

Compare the following:

Doctor 1

Me: **Doctor, I have an excruciating headache.**
Doctor 1: Here take this paracetamol. If you don't feel better in a week, call me again.

Doctor 2

Me: **Doctor, I have an excruciating headache.**
Doctor 2: Where exactly is the pain?
Me: **In my temples.**
Doctor 2: How long have you been suffering from these headaches?
Me: **For around 2 weeks now.**
Doctor 2: What time do you normally get these headaches?
Me: **First thing in the morning.**
Doctor 2: How much water do you currently drink per day?
Me: **Around a litre, I think.**

Doctor 2:	On a scale of 1-10, 10 being unbearable pain, what score would you use to describe your pain.
Me:	**7**
Doctor 2:	From what you have described I would recommend taking some paracetamol and upping your water intake to 2 at least 2 litres. If the pain persists, come and see me.

Which doctor would you rather see? Doctor 1 or Doctor 2?

Which doctor is better medically trained?

Which doctor has more experience?

We don't really know, doctor 1 could be more trained and have more experience than Doctor 2.

So why did you choose Doctor 2? What did he demonstrate that Doctor 1 did not?

He showed his credibility, took an interest in me, gave me absolute confidence that he was an expert in his field and he gave me trust. By just asking me some open-ended questions he gave me the perception that he was by far the better doctor.

FUN FACT

Only 13% of customers believe a salesperson can understand their needs.

Takeaway - Too many people in sales still don't get it. It's not about you. It all starts and stops with the buyer. Good sales professionals are like a doctor diagnosing a patient's illness. If you can't uncover your customer's problems and needs you don't stand a chance at selling them a solution.

So, what's the best way to remember the open-ended questions?

6 Bums On A Rugby Post

For visual readers, I would recommend the picture below that I describe as the "6 bums on a rugby post'. The rugby post (H) is the How and the 6 bums (W's) stand for: what, why, when, where, which and who.

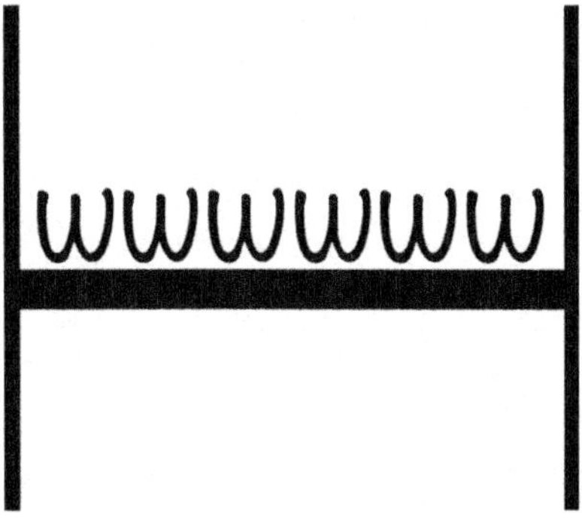

These types of questions should necessitate the client's participation in the conversation. This results in the client's attention being directed at you and away from any previous activity.

Examples of open-ended questions:

What is the main reason that made you decide to book this call?

Why else?

How would you like to see your business become more successful?

Why do you believe you need help?

Open-ended questions ensure that dialogue becomes less salesy and more like a genuine human to human conversation as you are showing genuine interest in their views and opinions.

Other Types Of Questions

Follow on questions:

As with everyday conversations these questions are a reply to your initial open question.

E.g. ***Why are you looking to start your own business?***

Because I feel stuck in my current job and I'm not earning enough money.

What's that like?

It's not good. I barely get to see my children.

How does that make you feel?

These follow up questions show that you have listened to the previous answer and now wish to get further information.

Decision-maker questions:

How will the decision be made?

Aside from yourself, who else gets involved in making the decision?

Is it that you need their permission to do this or do you just need to inform them of the decision you're making?

In the past how were these types of decisions made and who was involved?

What are the key priorities in order to make this decision?

Thought-provoking questions:

> ***What would you do if you lost your two biggest clients?***
>
> ***What processes and opportunities do you have in place to keep them?***
>
> ***Well from what you have told me you sound like the perfect client for us, what do you think?***

Closed-ended questions:

Asking closed-ended questions can be good too to clarify points, to get confirmation, to gain commitment and to close someone.

> ***If we take you on as a client and walk you through this result, are you going to be committed?***
>
> ***Would you like to pay in one go to get the discounted rate or break the payments into three instalments?***

ARQ Framework

Let me ask you a question. Have you ever been in a situation where you are asking questions and then you don't know what to say or ask next?

Chances are you were too busy trying to think what questions to ask next and you weren't actually listening to the other person and therefore we are not present.

We need to ensure we follow a framework to move the conversation in the right direction and that's why I have developed the ARQ framework which is essentially going to help you navigate your way through your sales conversation.

ARQ
Acknowledge
Repeat
Question

If you ask your prospect a question and they do not give you enough clarity to work with, then we use the ARQ framework to help you get to the truth.

We acknowledge the answer that they have given us, then we repeat it back to them and then we ask them the same question in a different way or a different question to help you move the conversation in a better direction and to uncover the real pains and problems.

Here's an example:

I hear you [first name], it sounds like what you are saying is that you would like to start a business. What I would really like to know is what are the top

two problems that you are facing that you need help with today?

This is a great tool to use if your prospect gives you a laid back response. Let's say for example you ask them "Why did you decide to book this call today?" and they reply "Oh because I was scrolling through Facebook and an ad popped up and I clicked on it". A typical salesperson would probably just move on. An elite seller would then stop to implement the **ARQ Framework.**

"I hear you [first name] it sounds like you saw our advert and was inspired to click to find out more. What I would really like to know is what is the main reason you decided to click to find out more."

Summary

To get our prospect to speak 5x more than we do we have to ask good, quality questions and we need to know what types of questions to be asking at different times.

One of the most powerful questions I use in my sales conversations contains just two words "What else?".

When I get an answer to my open-ended question I will normally follow up with "what else?" as typically the first answer a prospect will give you is never the real one. They are either telling you what they think you want to hear or they are protecting themselves from a 'salesperson' who they think may be trying to sell to them, con them or dupe them. It's also a great way of getting more information and building rapport by caring about your prospects' needs and by being a good listener.

EXERCISE

Before moving onto the next chapter, take some time to make a list of questions that would suit your current job or business. Practise asking them to family or friends and when you meet resistance implement the ARQ Framework

FUN FACT

The best time to cold call is between 4:00 and 5:00 PM.

Takeaway - Many sales reps make the mistake of calling during lunch hours. It turns out that most people are not receptive to a sales call when they are on their break, so call in the late afternoon.

9

Monetisation

I want to cover how much money you can really be making by implementing the systems and training early on in this book as it is key to have a realistically achievable target. I guarantee this will open your eyes to the amazing earning potential you can unlock by being an Elite Sales Specialist.

There are 3 main paths that an Elite Sales Specialist will be able to excel in and make an abundance of cash once they master the art of selling.

The BCE Routes

- Business Owner
- Consultant
- Employee

You may currently be operating in one of these areas or perhaps you are looking to branch out into one of these paths.

FUN FACT

Only 39% of salespeople intended to go into sales.

The great news is that my system and everything that you will learn in this book will set you up to be an elite specialist in any of the three paths, you can even take a mix of two or three of these routes.

I, for example, am a business owner who also consults for other leading experts.

Let's look at the earning potential for each path.

Business Owners

I will go as far as saying your earning potential as a business owner is uncapped because we are the limitations that we place on ourselves, it's all in our heads.

Your earning potential is technically uncapped, it all depends on how far you want to go with this, how far you want to go down the route of earning.

Our environments at times can limit how much we can earn. The people we hang around with, the products we sell in the marketplace we're selling in.

As a business owner, you have so much potential to sell on a global scale. A lot of us are just looking at localised business, we have so much more opportunity now globally to impact many more people, your products and services.

Every single business owner reading this book should have their eyes on adding at least another six figures into your business as an absolute minimum over the next twelve months.

Let's take a look at the pros and cons of being a business owner:

BUSINESS OWNERS	
PROS	**CONS**
Time Freedom Location Freedom Leave A Legacy Have Your Own Products Make More In A Day Than A Year	Generate/Pay For Your Leads Need To Build Your Brand Need To Create Systems Need To Run The Business Need To Deliver On Offer Business Costs

Independent Sales Specialists

An independent sales specialist is someone who will go off and sell other people's products and services and make a commission from that. I will be explaining further throughout this book exactly how to do that.

I'm going to be very conservative with this but over the next 12 months, you should set a target to be earning £60,000 as a minimum.

That's approximately £5,000 per month which is not difficult.

You could find one or two people who are selling a £25,000 package. You close that deal for each of them and you take a 10% commission as a minimum. That is two customers x £2,500 per month.

I personally saw a gap in the market in 2018 and made my money and grew to be one of the top independent sales specialists globally by selling for some of the top UK & US educational trainers like Liam Ryan for property education, Jessen James for Business & Marketing education and Ree Hurakan for E-Commerce education.

I consult for these experts and at a typical event of theirs make in excess of £5,000 in commission in either in-person interviews, Zoom calls & over the telephone in up to five hours of work in a single day. That's an average of £1,000 per hour.

They do the marketing, hire the venue, run and fund their teams and I come in and close their product and service for

£25,000 at 10% commission per deal and they provide the service or product to the customer.

Being an independent sales specialist can allow you to make some serious commission on a part-time basis which is why I still continue to do it to this day even though I have my own training business, plus it keeps me fresh and an expert in my field who practises what he preaches.

Let's take a look at the pros and cons of being an independent sales specialist:

INDEPENDENT SALES SPECIALISTS	
PROS	**CONS**
Warm Leads Time Freedom Location Freedom No Need To Deliver Product Make More In A Month Than In A Year	Results = Income No Control Over Delivery Need To Build Your Brand Need To Find The Right Gigs

Employee

If you are fresh into sales and you've never been in sales before then I recommend that getting a sales job is a great place to start after qualifying as an Elite Sales Specialist.

In your first year, you should be earning anything between £30,000 - £50,000 in your first year as an employee in sales.

Let's take a look at the pros and cons of being an employee in sales:

EMPLOYEE	
PROS	**CONS**
Consistent Income Experience Training & Support 9-5 Non-Monetary Benefits Employee Benefits	Linear Progression Limited Income Have A Boss Got To Work 9-5 (inflexible) 4-8 Weeks Annual Leave Trading Time For Lower Income

So all of the first-year estimated figures as a business owner, independent sales specialist or employee can progress to a hell of a lot more. I just wanted to keep the figures conservative and give averages of my clients income potentials after graduating as elite sales specialists.

FUN FACT

Nearly 13% of all the jobs in the UK (1 in 8) are full-time sales positions.

Takeaway - Today, salespeople are more important than ever and the sales profession is nothing like the negative stereotype of the past. Sales reps that are smart, nimble, and continuously developing the right skills have a bright future ahead. The takeaway for job seekers? Learn to sell.

FUN FACT

Over one trillion pounds (that's nine zeros) are spent annually on sales forces.

Takeaway - This is just another statistic that proves the emphasis businesses are making on their sales forces.

The Elite Sales Formula

Whatever route you take, one thing is for sure, you're going to make some serious money when you implement this correctly so it's really crucial we get clear on your money goal.

Think about how much money you want to make in the next 12 months. Whether you are a business owner, consultant or an employee or you are looking to start in one of these fields, write it down.

Now I'm going to ask you to take your number and double it. Yes, that's right, double those digits.

Something I learnt in the past is that if we set a goal of earning £50,000 a year and have the right plan and structure in place and work hard towards it then we are probably going to earn that £50,000. If you double that £50,000 target to be £100,000 and have the right structure in place and work hard to achieve it then we can do that too.

Worst case if we fall short of the new target and hit say £60,000 or £70,000 then we have still overachieved our original target.

> *'Shoot for the Moon, even if you miss you'll land among the stars.'*
>
> \- E.P. Rose

If the new number in front of you doesn't scare you then I am going to ask you to double it again until it does.

It's all well and good knowing how much you want to make in the next 12 months however, we now need to work out what your hourly rate is.

Take the figure you have written down and divide it by how many hours you would like to work per week and then divide it by how many weeks you would like to work per year to find out what your hourly rate will be.

A divided by B divided by C = your hourly rate

So let's say for example your goal is to earn £100,000 and you are happy to work 40 hours per week for 45 weeks of the year. Your hourly rate would be £55.55. If you were not earning £55.55 each hour you were working each week you would never reach your financial goal.

Now a question for you. Are you really going to be billing that amount minimum every hour?

No. You're not. You're going to have to spend time doing paperwork, doing procurement, travelling, in meetings etc.

So you can now see it's not really realistic to give yourself an hourly rate. This is why a lot of business owners and entrepreneurs give themselves an hourly rate and this is why they don't meet their financial targets.

A better way of getting to your financial target in sales is to work this out by selling X amount of units instead.

So let's say my target is to make £100,000 over the next 12 months and I have a product that is worth £500. I take my £100,000 target and divide it by my product value to work out how many £500 products I will need to sell in 12 months. In this case that works out to be 200 units.

Now I know those 200 units need to be sold over 12 months to get me to £100,000 let's work out what I need to sell per month.

I take the number of units I need to sell over the year and divide it by 12 as there are 12 months in a calendar year.

In this example, 200 divided by 12 will give me 16.6. Does selling 16 units a month sound easier than selling 200 per year?

There are 52 weeks in a year. If we take our yearly unit target of 200 and divide it by 52 we now only need to sell 3.8 units per week, call it 4 units.

So we have now gone from having to sell 16.6 units at £500 to make £100,000 to now only having to sell less than four.

That's even easier right?

Let's break this down even further.

200 units divided by 365 comes to 0.5. Just half a unit needs to be sold per day. So we basically need to sell 1 unit every other day.

Does that sound a lot more digestible and achievable than trying to build your business earning £55.55 every hour?

If you try and build your income out of an hourly rate you will never ever achieve your outcome in the time you said you were going to work.

I want you to now work out your financial goals using the following formula:

A (financial goal) divided by B (product/service) = C (units to be sold)

C (units to be sold) divided by D (working Days) = E (units to sell per day)

What are you going to sell to make that financial goal? Is it a £500 product, a £1,000 product, is it a £20,000 product?

If you're not a business owner and you don't have a product or service then I want you to work it out in commissions. How much commission per sale do you need to reach your financial goal?

So for example you might say you're not going to sell unless you get a minimum of £500 per deal. So If you were selling for someone at a 10% commission you would need to be selling a £5,000 product or service for someone else.

You should start to see that it is very doable now you just have to be clear on what your financial outcome is.

Be clear on what you are selling and at what price and then write down how many you need to sell per year, per month, per week and per day.

Where You Are & Where You Are Going

Where are you right now in your personal, professional and financial life?

Ask yourself:

- What does your personal life look like?
- What does your professional life look like?
- What does your business or career look like?
- What do your finances look like right now?

In order to move forward, you need to have total clarity on where you are right now. You can't possibly get to where you want to go unless you know where you are right now. It's just like getting in a car and programming the satellite navigation system to take you on a journey. When you put in your destination, what does it need to know in order to take you there? It needs to know where you are right now.

The SAT NAV can't possibly calibrate where you are going unless it knows where you are right now.

This is the problem with most people in the current age, they know where they want to go but they have no idea where they currently are now and then when they don't reach their destination they get angry and upset with themselves.

I speak to business owners and sales professionals all the time and they say things like "*I want to make 1 million pounds turnover in the next 12 months*" and I say to them "*Great! What was last year's turnover? How much are you currently making per month*", and they reply "*Oh, well I'm not really sure*".

Is making a million pounds really realistic? Do they actually have a vehicle to make a million over the next 12 months?

Take a moment to think about what has brought you to where you currently are today and what has brought you here. What I mean specifically by that is:

- What have you tried?
- What worked?
- What didn't work?
- Why didn't it work?
- What have you currently tried to solve your problems?

I see a common trend with successful people who over time stop being successful. It's mainly because they stop doing things that made them successful in the first place. Business owners, people at the top of their career ladder all seem to have a raging fire in their bellies when they start their business or climb their way to the top and it's that fire inside of them, that tenacity, that drive that helps them achieve what they have to date.

Sadly, what happens at times is that some of us lose that drive, we lose that hunger, we lose that tenacity for two reasons.

Number one: We get beaten up by the world, we get a little more tired, we start to lose faith and our momentum.

Number two: We get comfortable. Comfort is your biggest **ENEMY** when it comes to maintaining a successful life and even keeping strong relationships.

Please understand that if you want to be successful or even more successful then do not try to reinvent the wheel, don't stop doing the things you were doing in the first place or if you keep doing the same thing and nothing is changing then be aware that you need to do something different to get something different.

> **Insanity:** *"Doing the same thing over and over and expecting different results"*
>
> \- Albert Einstein

Be clear on what you have tried so far and what didn't work, you need to be obsessed with understanding why it didn't work.

Successful people look on the side of the cause and not on the side of the effect. We don't want to blame people, we need to take responsibility for negative outcomes. Ask yourself:

- What made that go wrong?
- Was I naive?
- How did I create this?
- Did I not try hard enough?
- Did I not know what to do?
- Did I put all of my eggs in one basket?
- Did I overleverage myself?

Once you have clarity on where you are and where you are going I can guarantee that you will vastly increase the chances of you living a happier, successful and more fulfilling life.

I regularly take 15 minutes or so to sit down with a pen and paper and to give myself total clarity on all areas of my life on where I am and where I am going.

Monetisation Is More Than Making Money

Most people want to get better at selling because they want to make more money. This may have been the main thing going through your mind as a driving force that led you to buy a copy of this book. Making money through sales is just the tip of the iceberg when it comes to the benefits of monetization through selling.

> **Monetization:** *The action or process of earning revenue from an asset, business, etc.*

We all want to be making more money of course but is it always only about making the money? I argue that the skill we need to learn in order to monetize is negotiation. Being an elite negotiator will not only help you add more money to your bank account but it will also help you save more money.

Instead of making money, see how you like the sound of some of the following:

- Receiving a better discount on your bills
- Saving money in your personal and business accounts
- Convincing people to do a job for you that will give you more time
- Reducing your rent/mortgage payments
- Negotiating on a car/property purchase
- Getting into a relationship with someone you like
- Getting a good business partner on board
- Hiring the building the best team
- Getting people to do things for you a lot faster and more efficiently
- Getting your kids to listen and do what they are told

Here is an example of a recent experience I had where it benefited me to be an Elite Sales Specialist outside a selling situation.

I had ordered a brand new mattress online off of a major furniture store (I won't say who) and on the day of the delivery I waited around and it never arrived. I had checked my emails to see that I had a message that my mattress had been successfully delivered. I went online to find a number to speak to one of the customer service agents as I knew that I was much more likely to get the deserved outcome with a human to human interaction in real-time rather than potentially messaging back and forth to various people over the space of a few days. I had a skip that was being collected at the end of the week so I had to ensure I got the result I needed as quickly as possible.

Whilst looking for the number off of a google search I came across a Facebook group with a number of people in it set up to complain about the service they received and their experiences with their customer service department and it seemed to me from their comments that they would go in trying to bully them and demand for what they want.

I put myself in the shoes of the customer service rep, most of the time they don't have any authority or know exactly what went on with the error, they're just on the phone trying to solve problems all day and mainly receive abuse and negativity.

So by understanding their position and telling them that I understand they probably don't have total authority and that they had no involvement in the delivery error and coming from a place of compassion I went on to be told "Wow, I don't think I've ever had a call like this in over 3 years because you're nice I'm going to get our warehouse to send you personal delivery this evening with your mattress and I will throw you in two pairs of duck feather pillows. I'll also email you a £50 gift voucher for the inconvenience".

Being elite at selling will have many impacts on not just your bank accounts, but your relationships with your loved ones, your happiness, your time, your freedom and your lifestyle.

Summary

When you become Elite at selling there are so many possibilities to monetise out of your skills. You can also use these skills and even consult for some businesses over the phone meaning you could operate from anywhere in the world.

Using the **Elite Sales Formula** will give you clarity on your realistic earning abilities and potential in sales. What I love about sales is that it is probably one of the safest sectors in any business. If a business was to start struggling, the last people to be let go would be from the sales team as they are the bloodline of the company that brings the money in.

You must be ultra clear on where you are now and where you are currently going in your business and personal life in order to clearly make plans to move forward.

Becoming an **Elite Sales Specialist** will help you in so many other areas of your life other than just making money from a job or a business. You will become a better negotiator, communicator and lover from mastering these life-changing skills.

EXERCISE

Before moving onto the next chapter, take time to implement the Elite Sales formula, even if you do not currently have a product or service just make one up that you would like to do in the future. Then spend 15 minutes or so working out where you are now and where you want to be in your business and personal life.

PART THREE

Performance

Now we have mastered our own psychology and our buyers' psychologies and we have learnt the processes behind being elite at selling, it's time to move on to my favourite step of the 3 P's.

To be elite at selling you need to follow a system and have a great script that gives you the authority in selling situations and pre-handles your prospects biggest concerns.

> *"By failing to prepare, you are preparing to fail."*
>
> *- Benjamin Franklin*

I am going to teach you my complete **7 Step Serving System** that I have used to close over £10 million in sales and that my clients have used to close well over £100+

million. The great thing about this system is that anybody can use it, anywhere, in person or over the phone and it can be used to sell anything to anybody.

Most sales professionals crumble and turn into a puddle when they are faced with an objection. In 86% of cases, the first objection we are given by a prospect is a lie, it's a neurological stall in their DNA which kicks in when they feel that they are being sold to which is where they will try to protect themselves from getting duped, conned, ripped off.

I am going to teach you my simple **LARA Method** that you can use with any objection to overcome it with ease and finesse which will put you back in control of the selling situation.

When it comes to closing the deal and asking for the money most sales professionals relay to the classic:

> *"How does that sound to you?"*
>
> *"Would you like to go ahead?"*

Once you master my **Two Doors Close** you will never use language like this again and your conversions and profits will skyrocket.

The sale does not end once you get the deal and collect the money. I am going to show you my complete follow-up method to ensure that your customers stay happy and content with their decision to invest with you and will ensure they will bring you referrals and come back to you in the future to reinvest or buy other products or services.

You are going to learn:

- The power-owning a mantra
- That an Elite Sales Specialist always puts commitment over the money
- The Complete **7 Step Serving System** to follow and close any deal
- The **LARA Method** to handle any objection thrown at you
- **The Two Doors Clos**e technique
- The post-sale **CROWN System** to maximise retention
- The power of the follow-up **Onboarding Call**
- The **Dr's Booking System** to lock in your appointments around your diary
- The best way to get free, hot, qualified leads - **Asking For A Referral**

10

The 7 Step Serving System Psychology

So whether you want to become an independent Elite Sales Specialist or you want to use these skills to grow your business then you need to know what it is that separates an elite seller from a typical salesperson.

- How is an Elite Sales Specialist to get to the truth with our prospects?
- How is an Elite Sales Specialist able to help the prospect make a decision that they may have shied away from in the past?

As well as having the mindset of an Elite Sales Specialist you must also have a system in place to take your prospect on a journey that will allow them to make the best next logical step for them which is to either buy your product or service or have clear steps on other solutions for them to take.

> *Approach each customer with the idea of helping him or her solve a problem or achieve a goal, not of selling a product or service.*
>
> *- Brian Tracy*

This is why I created the 7 Step Serving System which I am very excited to share with you now. This system can be used when selling one to one, for example: in person, on a phone call or zoom call.

There are elements of the system that can be used when selling one to many but for this part of the book, I'm focusing on a one to one consultation.

The main theme of **The 7 Step Serving System** can be remembered by the acronym **ICER**.

ICER

ICER	
1	Identify
2	Clarify
3	Establish
4	Reflect

Now when I say **ICER** I don't want you to decorate a cake, I want you to imagine this as your chunked up version of the sales call. I'm then going to chunk down through the following chapters on **The 7 Step Serving System**.

1. **Identify**
   The first step is to correctly identify the prospect's situation because if you haven't been able to correctly identify the real pains and problems they need to fix then how can you expect to solve it and know that it's the best decision for them?

2. **Clarify**
   The next step is to clarify, we want to determine what the prospect means by what they have said. As humans, we all have different models of the world. If you speak to a room full of people they will all hear what you have said but each person will process the information to their model of the world and they will clarify that information to their model which will be different from person to person. We want to ensure that with the information that we gathered, that we are on the same page as the prospect. Are we going to need to clarify that information? If so, do we need to know what we need to do about that? This brings us to step three.

3. **Establish**
   The next step is to establish what we have discovered and to organise that information into the best next steps for the prospect in terms of priority. We will be creating a list of outcomes that takes us into our fourth step.

4. **Reflect**
   The last step is to reflect on those outcomes and to help the prospect make a commitment and engage with those outcomes by following your actions.

Don't worry if this isn't making total sense right now, this is just a chunked up version of **The 7 Step Serving System** that I am going to now take you through step by step. See the **ICER** analogy as a birds-eye view of the system, think of **ICER** as the philosophy.

Own A Mantra

Now you know that I believe to truly sell you need to serve your prospect from a place of love. When it comes to selling this is the mantra that I and all of my Elite Sales Specialists adhere to in selling situations:

> *'The most important role of an Elite Sales Specialist is to help their prospects make the best logical step for their needs.'*
>
> *- Nick Staab*

Here is a sentence I always like to have in the back of my mind before I take a sales call or enter a face to face sales meeting:

> *'At the end of this call/meeting I will give this prospect complete clarity on their options and I will guide and help them make the best possible decision and take their next logical step as if I were in their shoes.'*

Create your own or stick it on the wall somewhere visible where to make your sales calls and be sure to read it out loud before dialling and after using the state scoring System (Chapter 3).

Commitment Over The Money

As an Elite Sales Specialist, we must come from a place of integrity and we must serve the prospect. Just because they have a credit card doesn't mean we are taking their money and accepting them into our program or selling them our product. We care more about their commitment than the money. This is super critical to understand this and it underpins everything we are about to go through.

This means if we are on a call and after discussing all of the options and we have gone through all of the steps I am about to take you through and we have discussed all of the options with the prospect and we feel that it's not the right decision for them to move forward, for whatever reason it may be that we then politely explain it to them that we don't believe that our solution is the next logical step for them to take.

We don't want to be blunt or rude here as this may hurt their feelings and ruin your relationship or have them tell their friends and loved ones or even leave an online review telling others to steer well clear of you. If we are politely declining them from buying from us then we need to advise on the next best steps for them to take to try and fix their problem.

Ok so (First Name), after our conversation today and going through my notes it sounds like you aren't ready to work with us yet.

I recommend that you either (*give them some tips, resources, etc*) **or you** (*give them some other tips, resources, etc*) **and then once you have what you need to in order to work with us we can speak again.**

Now, this may sound counterproductive, most sales training or typical salespeople are pushing for the sale. Push, push, push, sell the features, sell the benefits. They are in GET energy, get the money, get the sale.

An Elite Sales Specialist comes from a place of genuine care to help them make the best decision which will relate to happy customers who do not experience 'Buyer's Remorse' (something that I will cover later in the book).

Summary

So now that I have shared some of the mindset and philosophy an Elite Sales Specialist follows, let's get into **The 7 Step Serving System**.

Bear in mind that this is the exact 7 step system that I have used over and over again over the past few years to close millions of pounds worth of deals and my clients have used to increase sales conversions by up to 60%.

This is working time and time again right now and this is going to make you stand out from a typical salesperson and allow you to serve more people and make a lot more money.

REMEMBER

An elite seller will always prioritise commitment over getting the money.

EXERCISE

Before moving onto the next chapter, take some time to learn the ICER overview. Remember that this is just a chunked up birds-eye view of the 7 step serving system coming up next.

11

The 7 Step Serving System

There are just 7 steps that you will follow on your one to one sales calls or face to face sales meetings to make you elite at selling. We start by clarifying the call structure and expectations, then we find out about the prospects current situation, then we create goals for them, then we explain the consequences they will face if they don't tackle their problems now we will then certify if they are a good fit for our product or service, and if they are, then we move onto connecting the dots and then closing the deal.

You can plug and play what you are about to learn into your current business or if you're an independent sales specialist or you are looking to become one then you can use this framework to navigate yourself through any sales conversation.

For this process, we are going to assume that this is a sales call where a prospect has expressed an interest in your product or service. For example, maybe you, your company or employer has a website or social media adverts and a prospect has seen this and they have seen some content of your product or service. Then they have expressed interest and decided to book a call or fill in a form for more information.

So they have seen content, requested more information and now booked some time in your calendar to speak to you on a one-to-one call.

It's important to aim to have your phone consultations on Zoom or another video call platform if you can so that you can both see each other, you can share your screen to display information and you can build more trust and connection.

FUN FACT

63% of Sales Leaders believe that virtual meetings are just as or more effective than in-person meetings.

Now that we have set the scene let's get into it.

Step 1: Clarify

So the first step is to open the call and clarify with our prospects what they should expect to happen on the call. During this opening part of the conversation, we need to place the call and greet the prospect and then give them clarity on the agenda of the call and what the expected outcomes should be.

We want to keep this opening part of the conversation short and simple, the aim is to take no longer than 2-3 minutes here. We want to build rapport, trust and position ourselves as the expert.

Remember that you are the expert here and the prospect has come to you for advice and support. They are going to be responsive to your questions on this call if they trust you and see you as the expert so you need to take the lead and guide the flow of the call following the 7 steps.

Now a lot of salespeople may tell you that you need to start the call by building rapport, I go against the grain here and advise my clients not to force rapport building here.

I tell them to steer clear of forcing rapport building for two reasons. Firstly, because we need to open the call and give them clarity on what to expect straight away so we can build trust and position ourselves as the expert and authority figure. Secondly, because we sound like typical salespeople when we ask cliche rapport questions.

- *"How has your day been?"*
- *"What's the weather like where you are?"*
- *"Did you get up too much this weekend?"*

When we sound like a salesperson we trigger negative emotions from a customer's previous negative sales experiences or just remind them of the negative view they have of salespeople. It's almost like a loud high pitched siren goes off in their mind. Imagine it like an air raid siren.

'SALES ALERT! SALES ALERT!'

This phone call is a warm call which means the client is expecting your phone call and has a rough idea of the desired outcome and next steps. A cold call is when we call a lead who is not expecting a call from us. Now because the client is expecting us to call at the agreed time I simply start the call by getting straight to the point and not setting off sales triggers in their mind by behaving like a typical salesman.

Phase 1: Introduction

An elite seller's job at the start of this call is to build trust and connection whilst positioning themselves as an expert and taking control of the conversation, all while not sounding like a typical salesperson. It sounds like a big ask to do all of that but it's not when you don't overcook it; see the following intro I use to start my sales conversation and clarify the expectations and the desired outcomes of the call.

Hi is that (First Name)...

Yes, speaking, who's that?

It's Nick

Nick who?

Elite Sales Academy (use the brand/company name they will be familiar with)

Oh yes, Nick, How are you?

Great thanks, so (First Name) firstly thank you so much for taking my call. When you read my advert and booked in this call you would have read that there is an opportunity for you and me to have a discussion about your business strategy and the purpose of today's call is for me to ask you some questions and find out whether or not this is for you, AND if it is to get you enrolled on our training and that starts around 12 hundred pounds.

So, we have a lot to get through here, if you're ready we can go ahead and get started.

Notice how I give short answers and let them ask who I am rather than telling them everything as soon as they pick up the phone. This subconsciously starts giving me control of the conversation and will allow the client to have a positive mental flashback to when they saw you or your brand/company and the solution you are offering which can potentially fix their problem.

Even though I don't intentionally try to force rapport building here, If the prospect asks how I am doing or how my day has been I will answer their question and then set the scene asking if they are ready to go ahead and get started with the call.

This allows me to smoothly transition into giving the agenda for the call where I will clarify what they should expect on our call.

Something else you may have noticed which made you rub your eyes in disbelief was that I actually mentioned the price of my service at the start of the call. Yes, you did read that correctly.

So many salespeople these days try and teach that you never give out your prices until the very end, if the customer asks for the price you give them the whole **'Ahem (cough, cough) Yes sir, we will get to the price later for sure! Did I mention that with our program you're going to get... blah, blah, blah.'**

People are becoming a lot more aware and cautious of being sold to. If people ask for the price and you start dancing around the subject then this is just going to set the sales alarm off in their mind.

Transparency is key when it comes to selling. Being transparent and displaying your prices upfront removes any nasty shocks or surprises, it allows the prospect to build more trust with us and allows them to start thinking of how they will fund your product or service when you ask for their commitment or they are ready to buy it.

Phase 2: Clarify The Call

The prospect is probably wondering one of three things:

- What's going to happen on this call?
- How long is this call going to be?
- What's going to happen next?

We need to give the prospect clarity to help them understand exactly what is going to happen on this phone call, the potential outcomes and to let them know that if your solution is not right for them that you will try and help them solve their problem anyway.

Qualifying leads is a massive thing that typical sales people never do, they try to cram their products down their customers' thoughts as if it's exactly what they need when they don't even know their customers' real problems. This puts a wall up to a customer where they say to themselves that this salesperson only cares about making money off of me.

See the next example below of how I frame the call and give my customer clarity on what's going to happen on the call whilst positioning myself like an expert who really cares about their best interests (which at the end of the day is the most important thing when it comes to serving).

So (First Name), I want to be respectful of our time today. We have about 30 minutes or so to talk about the reason we are on this call and that is to see if we can help you grow your business.

So in order to determine if we can help you do that, I'm going to ask you some questions to find out what the current problems are so we can help you fix them.

Once we find out what is keeping you from growing your business, if I can help I will share with you exactly how you can get there, and if for some reason I can't I will let you know that and point you in the best direction for your next steps. But no matter what, you'll get massive clarity and value on this call and we will try and have a little fun, too.

Sounds good? [PAUSE]

Yes

GREAT, so before we jump in, we always record this call for training purposes. Now with that being said,

WHY did you decide to book the call? *(take good notes on the things they say that you will want to dive into - lots of verbal cues typically in this opening statement).*

Ok great, what else?

Ok, sounds like we have some things to talk about. Let me get up to speed on your current situation first.

That is a simple agenda that can be tailored to suit any business or product. You can see that I am very relaxed about the outcome and that either way whatever happens on this call I will help them move forward and that if they don't move forward with me that that is ok as well. This takes away the pressure and fearful feelings of obligation from your prospect.

Notice also how I will pause for agreement and acknowledgement. This shows I am giving my customers choices and freedom.

A top tip with pausing is to never ever talk over a customer when you ask questions or finish their sentences, even if you need to pause for 5 seconds until you get a response. A great trick I found was to physically cover my mouth with my hand whenever I asked a question and to only take it away to speak again after two seconds of silence once they have answered.

There is nothing worse than when you think someone has finished talking and you jump in to answer them and they have not finished talking.

When we ask why they booked the call we want to hear what they are looking to get out of the call and the problems they are facing. Be sure to take notes and always ask what else. 76% of the time the first reason prospects give us is never the true core reason they will be telling us what they think they want us to hear. Asking 'what else?' really gets your prospect thinking about the problems they are currently facing and the reasons why they need a solution to them and it should give you key pieces of ammunition to have up your sleeve. It is always better to ask what else rather than anything else, the latter is a closed question and it allows them to say no.

Now we are ready to move on to the next step and dig deep to find out all about the current situation they are in, the goals they have and the implications if they don't make a change to fix their problems.

Step 2: Current Situation

Now that we have given our customers clarity on what's going to happen on the call and the possible desired outcomes the next step is to understand how their problems are specifically causing pain in their life. What are the problems and how are they affecting their business or life?

When uncovering the current situation you need to:

- Seek to understand what motivated them to book this call.
- Understand their business/situation.
- Identify their pains and problem areas.
- Get extreme clarity along with the prospect in order to find the solution.

This is where you are going to be gaining an understanding of what your prospects' situation looks like. Once we do this we can determine if our service can help them to resolve their problem.

When uncovering your customer's situation you need to:

- Ask your customer quality questions to get clarity.
- Be a good listener.
- Use silence to let the pain land.

You are doing this so you can understand the specifics of what your customer doesn't like about their current situation.

The key here is to be a great listener and dig deep into these problems, we want to go multiple layers deep into their problems, not just take them on the surface level. We want to truly get deeper into the emotional levels of their current situation that is going to help us understand and help the prospect make the best decision.

This sales call will be a transfer of emotions. People make decisions based on their emotions and then they back up their emotional decisions with logic.

Elite Sales Specialists ask better questions and as a result, they get better answers.

Let me give you an example. Let's say your prospect is speaking about the dream of starting their own business or perhaps they have a business and they want to take it to the next level, why is that so important to them? Perhaps they are working a full-time job and they are looking to set up a business.

These would be the questions I would ask to uncover their current situation:

1. **What do you do for a living?**
2. **How many hours do you work a week including commuting time?**
3. **What do you take home each month? Is that your only source of income? How many people do you support on that income?**
4. **What don't you like about your job? (money, time, being at office, commute, stress)**
5. **Are you experiencing any issues financially? What would you like to do that you can't do because you don't have enough money?**
6. **What impact has this had on your relationships?** *(Partner, kids, social)*

7. **How would you rate your quality of life right now?** *(Happiness, fulfilment)*
8. **What are you missing out on because you are stuck in this situation?**
9. **What would you like to do if time or money wasn't an issue?**

In this uncover section we are asking questions and letting the customers answer and be heard. We want to follow up on their answers by digging deeper to get really specific and exacerbate the pain. We want to find the real pain behind the problem. It will most likely be a financial problem, *"stuck in a job I don't like" problem, "can't do something I want to do because of this problem" etc.*

The key here though is to let the prospect tell you about their life and the problems we are facing, we must never assume and tell them what we think they must be facing. Something a typical salesman will always try to tell them what their solution will do without listening to their pains and problems.

After a prospect answers a question we don't want to just acknowledge it and move on, we really want to dig deep and get them to explain more and give us more clarity on the impact the problems have on their lives and in other areas and how it makes them feel.

Here are some great follow-on questions I use after a prospect answers my initial questions throughout the uncover:

- Why do you think that is?
- How is that affecting your business/life?
- What's that like? How does that feel?
- Why is that so important to you?
- How long have you been dealing with this?
- What do you mean by that?
- Tell me more about that…
- Wow…*(down a tone)*
- Interesting...Hmm…
- Let's get more clarity around that…

We are also pre-closing future objections that may come up down the line. The biggest objections that come up in sales conversations are:

- Money
- Time
- Partner consent
- Risk
- Trust
- Shopping Around

Later in the book I will deep dive into these and how to handle them but by me asking about their job and sources of income can help me figure out if my solution is right for them and affordable, asking how many hours they work can give me an indication of how much time they have to implement this training, asking how many people they support allows me to find out if they have a partner where I can go on to ask questions like "Do they know you are on the call with me today?" "Are they supportive of you doing this?" "Are you the main decision-maker?" etc.

Don't forget to implement the ARQ Framework I taught you in chapter 8 if you get a laid back response from a question that you have asked. The ARQ Framework is to Agree, Reframe and then Question. Here's an example:

I hear you [first name], it sounds like what you are saying is that you would like to start a business. What I would really like to know is what are the top two problems that you are facing that you need help with today?

Now we have uncovered the pains we need to help the client paint a picture of how their future will look with our solution.

Step 3: Create Goals

Once we have uncovered the problems and pains the customer is facing, it's time to get them to visualize their future in their mind and paint themselves a picture of how their life will change by using your solution. You have identified their real reason for booking a call with you and you have identified what pains they are facing and what's going on in their life right now.

Next, we want to understand where they want to go and where they want to get to. We do this by helping them create their goals. I normally split this into two different fields and help them uncover both. Number one would be business goals (or something related to the product you are selling) and number two would be personal goals.

Business goals would include increasing revenue, growing a team, speed of growth, introducing new systems/departments, minimising loss, increasing marketing and influence.

Personal goals would include family, relationships, lifestyle, health career, educational, property or maybe spiritual goals.

As mentioned above this second goal may vary depending on what you are selling. If you were selling a car you would like to find out what kind of car they would like to drive, how many feats, what type of transmission, what size engine, what features it should have etc.

So from digging deep we can go through their goals through each of their categories. Essentially we want to understand why they want to achieve that goal. In some cases, a prospect may have a certain goal but they are unclear on the why and the steps they have to undertake to get there and without them being clear on this it's going to make it a lot tougher for them.

It's good to add here that you should never be in a position where you are creating the goals and creating them for them, an elite seller asks clever questions to make the prospect have the lightbulb moment themselves, that way they are more connected with the vision and they can start to visualize it happening and they can start to feel the good feelings that come up when they picture their future life having achieved their goals.

When we help them create their goals it is good for us to help them 'do the maths' as I call it where we will help them work out what they need to do to get to their goals.

Look at this example below where I will help create income goals with my prospect and help them do the math:

GOAL:

What is your monthly income goal? Why that number?

How soon do you want to be there?

DO THE MATH FOR THE GOAL:

At your current income, you will need to increase your sales to X to get there

What if you knew exactly how to close more deals and get your sales up to X? Do you think you could reach your monthly target?

Yes, I agree. That goal is very doable when you have the correct system in place and know what to do.

So, what do you think is the number one thing that is keeping you from getting to that goal of XYZ? (e.g. Don't know how)

Right. Without the knowledge of how to do this, it keeps you stuck, doesn't it?

So if they are currently earning X and they want to get to Y (let's say Y is doubling their current income of X) would you agree that this is going to help them be able to make improvements to their lifestyle?

If they can double their income they are going to be able to have a very different lifestyle and this is where we can help them create their personal goals. Doubling their income might allow them to be able to hire more team members allowing the prospect to step back and spend more time at home with their families. Maybe it would allow them to work from anywhere in the world.

We want to find out what the goals are and to really help the prospect paint a picture of what this will look like.

Let's say the prospect has a goal of purchasing a certain car. We want to ask them questions like:

- What make/model is the car?
- What colour is the car
- What do the interiors look like
- Have you been for a test drive with the GOAL?
- [IF YES] What did it feel like being behind the wheel? Revving the engine for the first time?

Let's look at another example of the client wanting to be able to take their family on a nice sunny vacation abroad:

- Where would you like to go?
- How is it going to feel having the sand between your toes, sipping on fresh coconut water, relaxing on your hammock watching the waves rolling in?
- What activities would you like to do with the kids?
- Great! Imagine the smiles on your kids' faces when you get to take them to the water park they have always wanted to go to.
- How's that going to make you feel?

We want to really get them to feel the emotions of achieving that goal.

After this point, we want to cover off the consequences of what they may face if they don't take action and purchase your product or service and identify any obstacles that may stop them from achieving these goals.

Step 4: Consequences

So now we have painted a picture with our clients on what their goals look like. This is where we start to look at the reasons why they haven't been able to do that so far and why they probably need our help to get them there and the consequences they will face if they don't do anything different.

We want to create a long list of obstacles for what exactly is currently getting in the way of them getting to their goals. We want to create a long list that will make the prospect say to themselves 'wow, I really have a lot of things stopping me, I really do need help.'

Let me give you an example:

So [first name] you're currently making £5,000 per month and you want to be selling £10,000 per month, tell me what's stopping you from achieving that on your own?

Now it could be that they don't have the knowledge, systems, time, the money to invest, their families it could be anything and each prospect will have their unique answer. An elite closer will take a long pause, be a good listener and ask questions to dig deep and find out more (just like we did in step 2: current situation). What's that like? Why do you think that is? How is that affecting your business? What else is stopping you from earning 10k?

From here we can formulate a long list of what's holding them back right now. You will see common trends here like lack of knowledge, support, not having the right systems in place and so on which is exactly what your product or service should be able to help them with to fix their problems if it is right for them.

Next, we want to find out what they have already tried to do to solve their problems, there is a chance that they may not have tried anything yet and you are the first person so it's good to ask them an open question to dig deep here.

Following on from the example above this is what I would ask next:

I hear you [first name] but if you were able to double your income to £10,000 it would change everything for you.

What have you tried so far to sell £10,000 per month?

How did that work?

Based on what they say you want to poke holes in what they have tried or thought of trying.

<u>Read books, asked friends, online videos:</u>

What results have you gotten from that?

Why hasn't that worked?

Do any of those help you to implement or guide you through your unique situations that come up?

Do they hold you accountable for the goal you have set and help you when you get stuck?

How will information equate to cash without action? If you don't know what action to take, how will you get to your goal?

Other programs/companies:

What programs have you done / companies have you used?

Why aren't you getting results?

What's missing from your current program that is keeping you stuck?

If new:

So let's take a look at what it takes to make this stuff work.

Do you think you need to have a process in place to be able to up your sales to £10,000 per month?

Do you think you need to know how to analyse potential opportunities correctly to ensure you take on the right deals with minimal risk and maximum income potential?

Right, so how are you going to do that? (they will most likely say that they don't know)

So if you don't know how to do that, what are the chances that you will be able to reach your income goal?

Now at this point, you should be cooking on gas, you will have positioned yourself as an expert and have the prospect in a position where they really feel that they need your help and that they have to buy your product or service to help them solve their solution. You now need to wrap it up and make them understand that now is the time to take action, if they leave this any longer they are just going to make their problems worse and that nothing will change for them and they will most likely never reach the goals that they listed to you.

If they have tried something:

So you've tried (insert what they tried) to fix it and nothing has worked because you are still not on track to be selling £10,000 per month and by continuing to do the same thing you can't expect it to change, right?

<u>Everyone:</u>

The difference between what you're doing and what our clients are doing is that you're working hard (insert job, time and effort to make a little money) and our clients have their money working for him while working a few hours.

What if you could learn the system that will enable you to double your income and then some within 6 months? How would that change things for you?

Right! A year from now your life could look totally different IF you start learning and implementing these strategies now.

[Insert features and USPs (unique selling points) of your product or service]

So [first name], being completely honest with yourself, how confident do you feel on a scale of 1-10 that you can figure this out on your own without any help and be earning you that £10,000 per month target?

(The prospect should give you a low number - If they give over a 4 then challenge them as if they knew how to do it and were confident then they would be doing it already)

Ok, no worries, most of our clients were around that mark too. I'm going to show you how you can do that in a few minutes.

You will have to get creative here and adapt your business/product/service into this formula. I have helped hundreds of clients from all different backgrounds with a range of different products and services create bespoke scripts following this model and creating a bespoke script is something that I offer in my advanced training.

Next, we want to ask the prospect consequence questions to help them realize what they are losing out on by having their problem and not fixing it.

Ok [first name], let's take a closer look at this. What are you losing out on by not knowing how to double your existing income? (Monetary and non-monetary).

So essentially you're losing out (what they said in a nutshell).

What is it worth to you to have (insert what they told you they want - for example, more time to spend with your loved ones, never have to worry about money ever again and live life on your own terms so you can do what you want when you want?)

But, if you keep doing this same thing, where are you going to be?

Right, and is this what you imagined for yourself?

So, how soon are you looking to change this?

Once we have highlighted the consequences the prospect will face if they don't do anything different it is time to move on to the next step where we will certify if the prospect is right for our training.

Step 5: Certify

So now we have outlined the consequences they will face if they don't do anything different or they don't invest in the right product, it is now time to certify if our solution is right for them. The main goals here are to find out if the prospect has the right mindset and the resources for change.

This is a really important step before we go onto the close as this is where we really want to get commitment from them that they can do this and that they are willing to do everything they can to make this happen. This commitment is great to take note of as when you go in to close if they backpedal and say it's not the right time you can take them back using **The Go Back Technique** (an objection handle technique I will show you later) and tell the prospect when you asked the question they gave you confirmation that now was the time to get started.

Another reason this step is vital to have in your sales script is that it gives you a chance to disqualify your lead if they are not the right fit. They may be suited for another product you offer or maybe it's just not the right step for them to take. Remember that we promised our prospect at the start of the call that we would work out if it was right for them or not.

Sometimes when we disqualify a lead they may actually fight back on us and try to convince us that they are the right person for the product or service and that can put us in a situation where they are 100% committed to going ahead with us if we are willing to take them on. It's up to us to use our best judgement here.

Ask yourself:

- Will they really benefit from our product or service?
- Do I want to potentially work with them as a customer?
- Is it morally correct for me to take their money?

We want to come from a place of service and our mission is to help our prospects make the best decisions based on their wants and needs. If you are going to feel guilty and lose sleep for selling them a solution that was not right for them then do not proceed with the sale.

Not only should it weigh on your moral compass if we sell our product or service to an unqualified lead, but no doubt the customer will not get the desired result, which could lead to a complaint, which then could lead to them telling all their friends and family how you ripped them off, which could then lead to a backlash of negative comments and reviews plastered all over the internet and have you left with a negative image to the rest of the world.

For most people to get from where they currently are to where they want to be is going to be different for them, it's going to be uncomfortable and it's going to be tough to get there. That's probably the reason that they aren't at the end result. In most cases, your product/service is going to act like a vehicle to get them from where they are to where they want to be, but they are still going to have to do their part of the work to get them to their desired result.

This is why it is key to get as much commitment and confirmation as we can to ensure that they are going to take the desired action and achieve their goals if they go ahead with your product or service.

As Elite Sales Specialists, we need to care more about getting their commitment than getting their money. Would you agree that when you are fully committed to doing something that you will find a way to make it work and when you're not really committed to achieving something you find excuses and distractions instead of getting the work done?

Gaining commitment will help your prospect believe they can achieve their goals with your solution and it will help them to visualise it happening in their future. I've always found with the clients I have sold to in the past that if they want something so badly and they can see it in their mind, feel it happening and they will commit to doing whatever it takes to make it happen then they will not care about the cost of what you are selling.

Let me show you an example of how I would certify my prospect caring on from my examples in the previous steps:

So [first name], before I pull back the curtains and go through the finer details of [your product/service] I want to make sure this is a good fit. The last thing we'd want is to take your money and not have the right results as it would not look good for our brand:

Are you open and willing to invest the time, money and energy into a solution if it gets you everything you want?

And If we show you how to fix this, are you ready to take action and start getting results now?

Can you commit up to 7 hours into training and growing your business per week? (After YES, educate how it's just 1 hour per day! Or a couple of hours on the weekends/their downtime - This depends on what you are selling obviously)

Great… And if we take you on as a graduate and walk you through to this result, are you going to be committed?

Ok, good because …we can't and won't work with everybody. It's not worth it for either of us if you aren't going to do your part of the work. Think about it like when you marry someone - that's the level of commitment from a mindset perspective we need.

Are you going to be an action taker? This is the most important. You'll be required to get the work done and take action. You'll need to be the type of person that does not procrastinate. We don't want the type of people that delay things for days. Really those are deal killers for us. Are you going to be the type of person that takes action?

Is there anything that will stop you from doing whatever it takes to grow your business that gives you more time, more freedom and passive income?

Have you thought about how you were planning on funding the mentoring and training to grow your business?'

Well from what you have told me you sound like the perfect client for us, what do you think?

At this point, we are looking for commitment and resourcefulness and therefore we will have a good idea of their situation.

Don't get hung up if they say money when we ask if anything will stop them, just observe and continue and if they say no when you ask them if they are prepared to invest in themselves then ask why. Take them back to their pains and based on their response decide if you need to end the call.

Now, this is a great part of the call to save you and your prospect each of your precious time and energy. If you need to end the call/meeting because they aren't the right fit, then you say:

"It sounds like you aren't ready to work with us yet, I recommend [give them some tips, resources, etc and invite them back to speak with you at a further date once they have what they need to be qualified]."

Step 6: Connect The Dots

So once you've gained the commitment, we now want to move onto the next step before we go onto the Close and that is to connect the dots.

Recap

We want to start connecting the dots by recapping everything with them that we have covered which is effectively our summary of their situation in a nutshell. We want the recap to briefly sum up problems and pain they are facing so the prospect can see everything clearly before them. We want the recap to be concise with a punch.

So just to recap, from what you have told me so far, you want to (insert goal/outcome they want), **but you can't do that because.** (insert problems and leverage from problems section, pain points).

Is that right? Is there anything else I missed?

Testimonial

Next in your sales presentation, I have found it is the best time to insert a testimonial, otherwise known as a success story. Customer testimonials can be a key content element because they are unbiased comments that prompt visitors to buy.

It is key to use a testimonial that links up to the prospect you are currently speaking to so they can relate, for example, if your prospect is working lots of hours and not earning enough money then use a testimonial about someone you have helped who was in a similar situation and all they have gone on to achieve now and how their life has changed and not someone who had their own business with lots of spare time who got on your solution for an additional stream of income.

Do you know what [first name], you really remind me of X (take them through how they started out like them and where they are now as a result of your product/ solution)

Solution

The goal of the next step is to help your prospect see that your solution is made for them. This is where you will go into detail on how your product or solution is going to help your prospect achieve their goals. You want to tie program descriptions back in with a question as you go through each one using the leverage of the problem.

Let me should you an example with our prospect looking to close more sales and double their income:

Just like (testimonial) we can definitely help you with this.

Here's what we are going to do to make (goal) happen.

The first thing we are going to do is teach you the 3 step system to generate more leads organically without using any of your own money. When you have the knowledge and you don't need to use your

own cash flow then you will have no obstacles getting in the way from you scaling your business in a short space of time, so you will be able to (make more money / have more time etc.)

Do you see that?

Great! Then we are going to show you how to close more sales, not only are we going to show you how to do this we will also write you your own scripts to follow.

We will show you exactly what to say to customers and how to say it so you have a constant flow of deals being closed and this will allow you to build your portfolio, maximise profits and generate cash flow so you have more time to (use their specific wants).

You will be elite at selling and have built something very special that you can be proud of. By the end of the year, we expect you to have doubled your income through sales to 10k that will be generating you £120k per year so you can (insert goal).

How does this all sound to you so far on a scale of 1-10?

Most of your prospects here will tell you they are a 10, if they say they are anything lower than a 10, why? Go back and answer questions for them to be confident in the solution.

Next, we move onto what features they will get from your product or service:

Great!

Here's how we work together to get you these results.

This is about mentorship, so that means we're not just showing you how to do it, we do it with you, this takes the guesswork out of the process.

We support you 1000%. This is a get it done program, you are implementing every step of the way.

In the next 10 minutes or so you are going to get sent login details to your own personal training portal. This portal contains the full step by step training and mentoring process. Everything you need to know to start, scale and grow a property business.

To help get you started and support you we are going to book you in for an on-boarding call in the next day or so with one of our Success Coaches. They will start mapping out your step by step plan and help you start your journey. They will book you

in for further consolidation calls and reviews along your journey.

Etc.

(Go on to list a total of 5-7 of the biggest offerings of your product or service)

Step 7: Close

So now we are finally here, the last step and we are about to go into our close and get the deal over the line. Now, this isn't always going to be plain sailing, even if we have done everything perfectly in the previous six steps we can not guarantee that your prospect is going to sign up without a fight.

In our next chapter, we are going to cover objections or stalls as I call them.

When we go in for the sale it's so important that we assume the sale. We think that everyone has the money to afford your product or service or at least they have the ability to get it.

Picture this: A tiger has escaped from the zoo and your family is out in the back garden and the tiger jumps over the fence. It starts to eye up your family for its next meal. Your neighbour pops his head out of the window next door armed with a tranquiliser gun. He used to be a sniper in the

Royal Marines so you know he would make the shot to put the tiger down.

He says "give me £5,000 and I will put the tiger to sleep for you", at this time the tiger is ready to pounce. Would you say "Sounds great... Could you just pop that down on an email and I will have a think about it."

I didn't think so, even if you didn't have £5,000 in the bank you would say yes and find a way to go out and find it.

The point I'm making here is that if your prospect is bought into your solution so badly that they have total confidence and conviction that your solution will solve their problems and you've built up enough desire that it's almost worth dying for them they will go for it.

If you do get objections at the close they either aren't willing, aren't sold or it isn't important enough to them to buy.

Let's carry on my example call and process into the close:

So [first name] does this give you the confidence you can reach your (financial goal)?

Great, well I am happy to go ahead and approve your application.

For your in-person training, we have dates on the 5th - 7th of June or the 25th - 27th of July, which one suits you best?

In total the investment is just £1,297, will you be paying on a Visa or Mastercard?

Notice here I did two big things. Firstly I did not close on the money my first time asking for commitment, I closed on getting them to book dates with me. Once you get buy-in and commitment on something you offer besides the money your chances of getting the money when asked have massively increased. Secondly, when I went in for both closes I did what's called a choice close.

A choice close is a multistep process designed to get an affirmative answer or commitment from your customer, often with regards to making an appointment and starting the sales process. When using the choice close, you are not asking a yes or no question, you are asking an either-or question. In theory, saying No to this question isn't really an option.

Using a choice close is so much stronger than other salespeople I hear asking 'Would you like to go ahead?"

Something key to note also is the power of the pause. When you ask your closing question you just have to pause afterwards and totally refrain from saying anything, even if your prospect takes 30 seconds to open their mouth you do not say a word. They are going through their buying process and if you interrupt them or take them off course then you could crush the sale and leave them feeling like they "need to go away and think about it.".

You can't do this in person but if you're on a phone call literally cover your mouth with your hand and do this until the prospect speaks and finishes their sentence.

Now hopefully you have closed the sale and you are taking their payment, after that it will be time to finish your call or meeting by quantifying the next steps. Chances are though that you would have come up against an objection or a stall that needs overcoming. Let's move on handling those objections before going on laying out the prospects' next steps.

Summary

So there we have the 7 Step Serving Formula which you can use in any selling situation to sell any service or product flawlessly. I have personally used and fine-tuned this system to close over 10 million pounds in sales and my personal clients have used this formula collectively to close over 100 million pounds in sales.

The trick here is to trust the process and just have so much confidence and belief in your product and this system so that your prospects will become compelled to invest their time, money and energy into you.

Practise makes **Permanent**

You will need to practise this in the real world and with your team or solo to get it fine-tuned and natural. A great tip I recommend while on a phone call or in a meeting is to have the 7 steps written down and spread across the length of an A4 page as a visual guide and to help you take notes in each section.

Here is an example:

Clarify

Current Situation

Create Goals

Consequences

Certify

Connect The Dots

Close

EXERCISE

Before moving onto the next chapter, take some time to learn the 7 Step Serving System.

Practise with a team member or with a family or friend, be sure to swap roles so you can feel the experience of being a customer on the receiving end.

12

Overcoming Objections

You are probably going to meet some objections or stalls as I like to call them because that's what they really are. When a prospect is giving you an objection they are stalling from giving you a yes. Maybe they are giving you a genuine reason why they can't do this, maybe they are politely trying to say no without giving you the real reason.

Objections are nothing to fear, every prospect you speak to has sales objections or reasons they're hesitant to buy your product. Sales objections are pretty much unavoidable because if the buyer didn't have reservations about your solution's price, value, relevance to their situation, or their purchasing ability, they probably would have already bought it.

The main thing you can do when handling objections to increase your chances of closing is to just have total confidence and conviction in your response. This comes with practice and having a bulletproof objection handle method in place that I'm now going to show you.

Objection Handling

Objection handling is a natural part of selling, but it can be a significant roadblock when you're trying to move prospects through the pipeline. You might even be tempted to accept the objections and send a breakup email straightaway. This is especially true if the objection seems highly reasonable based on what you know of the prospect's business.

To be successful, sales reps must learn how to both discover and resolve these objections. When objections arise, it isn't the time to give up, it's time to re-emphasize your product's value.

WHAT IS OBJECTION HANDLING?

Objection handling is when a prospect presents a concern about the product/service a salesperson is selling, and the salesperson responds in a way that alleviates those concerns and allows the deal to move forward. Objections are generally around price, product fit, or competitors. Sometimes, the objection is a good old-fashioned brush-off.

Objection handling means responding to the prospect in a way that changes their mind or alleviates their concerns.

Some salespeople argue with their prospects or try to pressure them into backing down, but this isn't true objection handling. When pressured prospects typically end up more convinced than ever of their position and they lose the trust and rapport they've built up with the salesperson.

Instead of telling your prospect, they're wrong, as an elite sales specialist, it's our job to help them come to a different conclusion of their own accord. And if you can't persuade them, that's a good sign they're potentially a poor fit.

I have created a simple 4 step method that I use and teach for handling any objection and I call it the **LARA** method.

The LARA Method

A proven and effective method for objection handling I created is called LARA involving four steps: **L**isten, **A**ppreciate, **R**elate and **A**ccelerate.

Listen

When confronted with an objection, the first requirement is to listen to the objection. This demonstrates to your customer that you are interested in their concern and care about what they have to say.

Appreciate

The next step is to agree & appreciate your customer's concern. This is where you demonstrate you have been actively listening. Remember the saying: 'The customer is always right.' An acknowledgement can be something as simple as a head nod or a restatement of the issue. A sincere acknowledgement can circumvent an argument and have a calming effect. Sometimes, your customers just want to know that they are being heard.

Relate

The third step is to explore the concerns underlying your customer's objection and relate them back to them. You want to find a solution and solve it for them.

Accelerate

The last step is to ask a question to get back on track to your desired outcome.

Here are some examples of the LARA method in action:

"I need to speak to my partner."

"I appreciate that you need to speak to your partner, most of our clients feel the same when we make the offer. What do you think your partner would

need to hear to make them feel that this is the best decision you've ever made?

Great, that's exactly what we're going to teach you in our training. As we have limited spaces and I don't want you to miss out, let's get your deposit down, if they're totally not on board we will give you your money back. Will you pay on a Visa or Mastercard?"

"I'm a bit busy now, let me get back to you."

"I appreciate that you're busy, so I will keep this brief. What date would you like to come to our event, June or July?"

"I'm not sure I can afford it at the moment"

"I appreciate that you can't afford it, what would you need to learn from our training to make it the most invaluable thing you ever paid for?

Great, that's exactly what we will teach you, sign up for our training and you will never have to worry about not being able to afford training again. We offer a payment plan option where we can reduce the fees to £495 per month over 3 payments. Will you be paying on a Visa or Mastercard?"

"I would love to go ahead but I'm not sure I will get the same results as your other clients."

"I totally appreciate that, results are critical to us. What result would you need for this to be the greatest investment you have ever made?"

(If their answer is achievable) **That's exactly what we are going to teach you over the 3 days. Would you like to come in June or July?**

Here are just some examples and the great thing about this method is that I don't need to have a rigid script that I use on each prospect's objection, their objection is completely unique to them and I just follow the LARA method on the spot to make it unique and personal to the prospect.

FUN FACT

92% of sales professionals give up after the third objection, but 80% of prospects say no four times before they say yes.

It is important that we keep handling objections and after 3 attempts resulting in an objection, we switch to something I call the Go Back Technique.

The Go Back Technique

With the information you gathered when following **The 7 Step System** you will have so much ammunition up your sleeve from their pains and goals to take them back to. I employ the **Go Back Technique** after I receive three objections in a row.

If I continuously use the **LARA** method it will get familiar with the prospect and could come across salesy. I think of the time to employ the **Go Back Technique** being compared to a game of baseball. 3 strikes and you're out! Well.. not in our case.

For example, if a prospect told you that they hate their job and they can't wait to leave and you offer them a solution which they say they are 100% committed to and when you go to close you handle 2 objections using the **LARA** method and then they say that they want to think about it you can take them back to the pain and goals you uncovered in the **7 Step Serving System** that you can utilize in your objection handle.

> **"I totally appreciate that you want to think about it, Let's go back a minute [first name], earlier you told me that you couldn't wait to leave your job and you wanted to earn more money so you could spend more time with your kids and finally take little Jennie to Disneyland as you've always promised her. Is that still correct?**

You're only going to get a yes here and you can continue to go deeper or use a testimonial here from a previous client who was in a similar situation to them or who had a similar objection when it came to closing them and share the results they have achieved and how their life has transformed since taking action.

Once you've brought the prospect back into their pain and pleasure and they should be in a position to be closed and I follow up with something I created which I call **The Two Doors Close.**

The Two Doors Close

I love this close, I find it to be so powerful when followed up from the Go Back technique. **The Two Doors Close** is effectively where I get the prospect to close their eyes and visualise that they are in a dark room with nothing but two closed doors in front of them. They are going to need to choose what door they enter.

Door 1: You enter this door and you stay exactly where you were. You are still experiencing [pains] and you won't be able to achieve [goals] and nothing is going to change for you and there is a possibility that it could get worse.

Door 2: You enter this door and you use our [product/service]. Your [pains] will end and you will achieve your [goals] and you finally feel [emotions they described]

Let's look at it in action following on from my example with the **Go Back Technique**:

[First name] I want you to visualise something with me. Close your eyes for a minute. Ok picture this, you're in a pitch-black room and you can only see two doors in front of you and you need to now make a choice of which one you will enter.

If you enter the first door and you're going to stay exactly where you are. You are still stuck in the accountancy job that you hate, living paycheck to paycheck feeling miserable. You're not going to have that freedom to spend more time with your family, be able to do the school runs with Jennie and it's unlikely you will ever be able to take her to Disneyland like she always dreamed.

Or you enter the second door where we show you the exact systems and support you in starting your own business. You will be able to replace your income and then some so you can come out of your job and be your own boss, wake up when you want to wake up, not when the alarm clock tells you and like you said earlier this will make you finally feel free and you would be happier than you've ever been.

Which door are you going to take [first name]

Great, let's make this happen. The investment is just £1,297, will you be paying on a Visa or Mastercard?

You Can't Win Them All

I'm sorry to tell you this but you are not going to close every sale, However, following this sequence will massively increase your chances of doing so. If you follow the sequence and you just can't get commitment from them you should be in a position where your gut will tell you if they are being genuine and then we will allow them to go away but we will always have a follow-up call or meeting booked there and then in the diary in the next day or two.

If they need to think about it, do their research, speak to their partner or whatever reason they gave you that you couldn't overcome on the initial call or meeting then they do not need a week to make these decisions.

On average each day that you leave a prospect who declined an offer that you have pitched, the chance of them doing business with you will decrease by 50% each day. This is mainly down to their fear kicking in, talking themselves out of it and allowing other people's opinions to impact their decision making.

You are going to need to book in a follow-up call using something I have created which I call **The Dr's Booking System**. I'm going to explain this in the next chapter as

I explain what happens next after the close or if we can't close the prospect.

Summary

No matter how well we do in the **7 Step Serving System** we are almost always going to meet objections. Remember to stay calm, these are just their concerns and have nothing to do with you.

You will use the **LARA** method and ask responsive questions based on their objection to help them overcome their fear. When you use the LARA method another objection may come up, so keep going through them until the third objection.

This is where you will use the **Go Back** technique to take them back to their pains and their pleasure and then I finish with **The Two Door Close.**

You're not going to be able to close every prospect you speak with but your chances will skyrocket following these systems.

Now we know how to flawlessly handle objections with confidence and conviction. Let's move to the next steps we have to take if the prospect did or did **not sign up.**

EXERCISE

Before moving onto the next chapter, take some time to practise objection handling using the LARA Method, the Go Back Technique and the Two Doors Close. There are 2 ways I recommended practising this:

1. *Take Cue Cards and write down all the objections on each card that you can think of that your customers have used on you or if you don't have customers think of the most common ones you could face. Shuffle the cards and then play a game where you deal a cue card and you handle the objections using the three techniques.*
2. *Practice role-playing with someone else and go through the techniques. Be sure to swap roles so you can experience the power of having these techniques used on you.*

13

The Next Steps

Now you have finished the sale, now is not the time to waffle and veer off track. You still have 5 final jobs to do to ensure that your deal sticks and your prospect receives the most value from your product and service and they go on to future business with you and bring you referrals.

The CROWN System

I have created a 5 step after-sale system I call CROWN. You will feel like a King or Queen in your field when you use the following after-sale system:

1. Congratulate - Make your prospect aware that they have made the best decision and thank them for their business.
2. Resistance - Honesty and transparency are key here, bring up the elephant in the room and tell your customer that they may feel buyer's remorse as soon as this call or meeting ends.

3. **O**ther People - Once again we are being honest with our prospect here and pre addressing that other people may install their own fears or doubts into you if they find out about this decision. It can be that other people are envious of your customer changing their lives or their closest loved ones trying to protect them and their money. You must address as this can be one of the biggest factors to post-sale cancellations
4. **W**hy - Get them to write down the reasons why they have made this decision and how their life is going to change when they get the desired result. That way if fear kicks in or other people try to negatively influence their decision to buy from you, they can go back to read their reasons for doing this to reinforce that they have made the best decision.
5. **N**ext steps - be clear on the next steps and be clear on exactly what's going to happen after this phone call or meeting ends. There is nothing worse than buying something and not being clear on what happens next. This could be not getting a confirmation email or being told a delivery date for your purchase. Not being given next steps causes a buyer's fear to skyrocket. Your buyer may ask themselves the following questions:

- *"Have I been duped?"*
- *"I don't have a clue what I need to do now"*
- *"It doesn't look like I'm going to get my order, better warn others and leave a 1* review on Trustpilot."*

I can't stress enough that an Elite Sales Specialist is always transparent and upfront. Honesty is the best policy, and you are doing your customer a dis-service and limiting your selling potential if you don't bring up the negatives.

Your prospect will be grateful as chances are they are on cloud nine at the point of sale with the job you have done.

Have you ever had a time in your life where you ever bought something of value, got home that night and laid in bed and thought to yourself: "*Crap, why did I buy that?*"

How about a time where you told a loved one of a purchase you made all happy and they said: "*What did you go and buy that for? That seems a bit expensive? Can you really afford it?*"

The problem with other people influencing your buyers is that nine times out of ten they weren't there when they brought it, they don't fully understand your product or service and how the reward will well outweigh the risk and they probably don't know that you qualified your buyer.

Addressing the problems will minimise the potential of them becoming problems to your buyers.

Let's take a look at the **CROWN** System being used in this example following up from the sale in the previous chapters:

CONGRATULATIONS [first name]!

I'm super excited for you. This is going to be an amazing journey. You have just given yourself a huge gift.

I want to be totally honest and transparent with you here. The thing to keep in mind is that when you make a decision to change your life, a lot of RESISTANCE and stuff can come up.

OTHER PEOPLE can also mean well, but they also can't see what you see, so sometimes they want to input their own fears or doubts onto you. It is imperative that you don't allow anyone else to change your path. This is your life and you get to choose how awesome it's going to be. The only thing that will change you from having more time, more freedom, more money is you deciding that you are not going to have it and allow others to create doubt in you.

So, take a moment and write down WHY you are doing this so you can look back on it and remember your big WHY and see how far you have come. So if you do feel a bit fearful or someone else's opinion negatively influences you then recognize that is normal and then go back and read the WHY that you wrote down.

If something comes up for you, reach out to me or the team, we are here to support you all the way, ok?

Great, now I want to run you through the NEXT STEPS. In the next 5 minutes, you are going to be emailed out your terms and conditions and all of your login details to your members portal. Please make sure you look through these and you can log in and start the training ok.

What I will do now is book you in for your onboarding session in the next day or two where I will take you through the members' area, chat about your plan and walk you through all the next steps. Ok, so I've got tomorrow or Wednesday which suits you best?

Great, Morning or Afternoon?

10am or 11:30am?

Amazing that's all booked in, you're going to get a calendar invite coming through now. Have you got it?

Great I can't wait to catch up with you at [date and time]

While I have you, Who else do you know who would possibly be more interested in [your solution]?

Thanks! Have a great day, well done now go and celebrate.

Follow this system and you will ensure that your customer will feel at ease and be grateful that you have addressed the elephants in the room. They will have a clear plan on the next steps and be sure to look back on the reasons why they have made this investment and feel comfortable reaching out to you on a potential dark day.

We will now deep dive into the power of the follow up on-boarding call.

The Onboarding Call

The onboarding call is a powerful call that is 100% worth the time to implement whether it be done by yourself or with one of your team members.

The purpose of the onboarding call is to mainly ensure that your customer is satisfied with their purchase and to answer any questions or issues that may have been raised by the customer since their purchase.

Depending on your business and product and services I would be sure to create a checklist of all the things you would like to cover with a customer to ensure they are getting the most out of their purchase and to cover the typical main issues that may arise for others.

An example of my checklist for somebody who has enrolled on my 3-day Elite Sales Bootcamp training would be:

1. Thank them for their purchase
2. Tell them the reason for this call is to ensure they are getting the maximum benefits available out of their purchase and to answer any questions they may have
3. Ask them to remind me why they have invested their time, money and energy into my solution
4. Go through a product checklist, in our case:
    - Make sure they have received the welcome email, terms and conditions, log in details to their members portal and the link to join the private Facebook group.
    - If they have not already, get them to go into the Facebook group and help write a post to introduce themselves.
    - Get them to log into their members' training portal and then through each section step by step getting clarity that they are clear with it and understand each part.
5. Give them the dates, location, timings and information for our 3day in-person training events and get them booked in on the earliest logical option which suits them.
6. Setting them some actions to work on.
7. Asking for anything they need help on.
8. Quantifying the next steps or point of contact if needed

9. Asking for a referral again

Make sure you book in the Onboarding call follow up at the earliest convenience for both parties when you are at the end of your sales call/meeting, the longer you leave a customer alone the higher chances that they may experience buyers remorse or be influenced by someone else that they made a bad choice buying their product or service.

FUN FACT

Retaining current customers is 6 to 7 times less costly than acquiring new ones.

Takeaways - Pay attention to your existing customers. The fact that they are engaged with your brand gives you an advantage that you'd be mistaken not to capitalize on. This is all about account management, up-selling and cross-selling.

Make sure that when you go to book an Onboarding call with your customer that you give them two possible choices of booking options, which is something I call the **Dr's Booking System.**

The Dr's Booking System

Rather than saying to your prospect "ok well let's catch up later in the week sometime, I'll give you a call" it's much more beneficial to book in an agreed time with a prospect for a follow-up call as you want the chances of them picking up the phone and speaking to you at the agreed time to be as high as possible.

With the **Dr's Booking System** I am simply giving the prospect two choice options to get a higher chance of commitment and it also helps you work around your diary.

I call it the **Dr's Booking System** as when you book a Dr's appointment this is the exact method I have found that they use in my experience.

Let me show you an example assuming the day of the consultation I'm finishing is a Monday:

So [**First name**] **let's get this call booked in, please bear with me whilst I check my diary** [**Pause**]

Ok, so I've got tomorrow or Wednesday which suits you best?

Tomorrow

Great, Morning or Afternoon?

Afternoon

3 pm or 4 pm?

4 pm

Amazing that's all booked in, you're going to get a calendar invite coming through now. Have you got it?

Yes

Great! I'll also send a summary of our meeting today and attach our offer in. Any urgent questions reply to the email or give me a call, any other questions make a note and I'll answer them tomorrow at 4 pm.

FUN FACT

*42% of people would be encouraged to make a purchase if the sales rep called back at an agreed-upon, specified tim*e.

Now we have our onboarding call booked in the diary we go onto one of the most powerful ways for you to get free hot qualified leads into your businesses that most sales professionals never do, and that is to ask for referrals.

Ask For A Referral

Asking for a referral is an extremely powerful lead generation strategy that most sales professionals do not do The advantage of asking a buyer for a referral is that the referral will know that their referrer has invested into the product and with both knowing your referrer you will have built plenty of things to talk about with your new referral.

The great thing about asking for a referral is when done properly, this can even be asked to non-buyers. Asking for a referral is a must at the end of every sales call or sales conversation to help you build your pipeline with hot leads which don't cost you a penny.

Before I go, who else do you possibly know who (insert your solution) needs help with selling and would like to double their income?

Great! How can you connect us right now?

Now, most humans need to do things at the moment or they just don't get done. I know that I will tell someone I am going to do something but then the phone will ring or I will get distracted and I will forget about the task I told someone I was going to do.

The same goes for your prospects, unless they do it then they are likely to forget. So if they answer "I know my cousin Paul is, I will give him your details" I would reply "Great, I'm sure you would but what most of my clients do is send a group message introducing us both just in case something comes up and they forget. Pop me on loudspeaker and let's get that done"

FUN FACT

Salespeople who actively seek out and exploit referrals earn 4 to 5 times more than those who don't.

Takeaway - Referral-based selling is a surefire recipe for success. A referred customer is already pre-sold on the credibility of the salesperson, product and company which makes these types of opportunities the warmest sales leads.

FUN FACT

91% of customers say they'd give referrals. Only 11% of salespeople ask for referrals.

Takeaway: If you are making this mistake, you are wasting precious opportunities. All you have to do is ask! What's the worst that can happen?

Summary

Quantifying the next steps after you have sold your product or service with a client is key.

Do what others do not and address the elephant in the room and bring up the buyer's remorse they may feel or the potential sabotage they may encounter from other people and loved ones on their decision to buy from you.

Use the **CROWN system** to ensure that you can cover all of the hindering thoughts a prospect may be having or have in the coming days and then quantify the next steps with them.

Book in an **Onboarding Call** at your earliest convenience using the **Drs Booking System** to ensure your customer is happy and making the most of your product and service to ensure they will not want to cancel or get a refund and that they will buy from you directly time and time again.

Always **Ask For A Referral** at the end of your selling situation, even if they don't buy.

EXERCISE

Before moving onto the next chapter, take some time to practise the end of your selling situation by using the CROWN System.

Practice role-playing with someone else and go through the Crown System. Be sure to swap roles so you can experience the power of having this system used on you.

Conclusion

It is helpful to know that when you follow my 3 P's System from start to finish and you have served your prospect, overcame all objections with ease and finesse and turned them from freezing cold to red hot that people will lie to you, make excuses and buy themselves time. It is hard-wired in their DNA when in selling situations and no matter how amazing you have done following the system, you must be prepared for it.

When you are in a selling situation with your prospect and you know them and understand them by knowing:

1. The problems they are facing linked to your product or service
2. The solutions they will gain linked to your product or service
3. What they need to do to solve their problems
4. That both parties know, like and trust each other

And that you have given your prospect all of the logical information and that you have discussed:

- The possible obstacles
- The possible risks
- The possible implications
- The possible problems
- Who else may be a decision-maker
- That you are talking to the final decision maker
- The next steps

Then you have earned the right to close them if you are certain that your product is the best next logical step for them.

Incorporate the 3 P's and follow the 7 Step Serving System in all selling situations and not only will your conversions and income skyrocket but so will will your confidence, negotiation and communication skills.

Implement the teachings from this book and you will become a better salesperson, mother, father, brother, sister, son, daughter, friend, colleague, lover and just a better person as a whole. I guarantee it.

You will master the art of selling.

It is now your job to implement what you have learned and making it your mission to make your mark in the world by serving as many people as you can ethically with confidence and conviction.

To become a master at anything though it takes constant practice and implementation. If you were to study any competing athlete you will see that even though they have learnt how to be an expert at what to do, they constantly practise, invest in mentors and trainers and make their skill an obsession to truly be elite at it.

Practise this every day.

Follow me on Facebook to get daily reminders and teachings: Nick Staab.

Ask to join my free Facebook community: AFL Elite Sales Facebook Community.

Now, it's over to you.

Key Reminders

Do not overcook it. Selling does not need to be underhand, complex or different in any way.

An elite seller speaks 20% of the time and listens 80%. Ask good quality questions and be a good listener.

PAUSE, use silence to let the pain land. When you ask a question, cover your month (if on the phone), do not speak until your prospect has answered.

Be yourself. Nobody can be a better YOU than YOU can. Follow these teachings but never try to imitate somebody else. If you naturally like being humorous, throw in some humour. If you like dropping mind-blowing facts then use data and information in your pitches.

Be open and honest from the start of a selling situation. Set the scene and structure of the call and even mention your cost. Your prospects will love you for this as it's the opposite of most other sales professionals out there.

Say NO to people who do not qualify and who will not benefit from your product or service.

Do not be scared to ask for the money or the deal. If you have followed the steps then you have earned the right.

You are your biggest asset. Invest into yourself.

Get sales training, role-play daily, remind yourself of the sales process which, when repeated, gets massive results time and time again.

FUN FACT

Continuous training gives 50% higher net sales per employee in sales jobs.

Takeaway - The impact of sales training is hard to measure, so many sales leaders doubt its effectiveness. The truth is that investing in your people has a positive impact on your organization, even if that impact is not clearly seen in sales results immediately following a training program.

Become An Elite Sales Specialist

We have opened our 1-2-1 and group training across the UK and we are looking to train and mentor the next Elite Sales Specialists.

Join the public Facebook group the AFL Elite Sales Facebook Community and send me a direct message showing your interest.

I run a three-day in-person training called the Elite Sales Bootcamp with my amazing business partner Liam Ryan.

We only work with limited people on a monthly basis and getting a place on the training is application only. Like this book preaches, I only want to work with candidates who are the right fit so we will need to have a discussion to make sure that our training will be your logical best next step.

You will leave the three-day training with your own bespoke 7 step serving script that you or your team needs to close hot, qualified leads every time.

The Author

Nick Staab is the Co-Founder of the Elite Sales Academy, one of the UK's leading sales training companies that have helped thousands of sales professionals from all different industries become elite at selling and closing.

Having closed over 8 figures worth of sales deals collectively, he's a much sought after speaker, trainer and sales coach. From starting his sales journey by canvassing door to door for an energy company in Australia and becoming their top seller out of over 100 team members in just three months to go on to sell for the biggest education companies in the UK, Nick has always known that the secret art of selling is to serve his clients.

Nick put his life's work into creating a simple system called the 3 P's that anybody can learn and master to become elite at selling in any sector or industry. Nick is becoming the go-to guy for business owners and sales professionals who want to go to the next level.

Find out more at:

http://nickstaabcoach.com
www.Facebook/groups/elitesalescommunity
https://www.facebook.com/NickStaabCoach
www.linkedin.com/in/nickstaabcoach
Instagram: nick staab coach

Printed in Great Britain
by Amazon

66904495R00139